FACING MICHAEL JORDAN

FACING MICHAEL JORDAN

PLAYERS RECALL THE GREATEST
BASKETBALL PLAYER WHO EVER LIVED

EDITED BY SEAN DEVENEY

WITH KENT McDILL

SPORTS
PUBLISHING

Sports Publishing books may be purchased in bulk at special discounts for sales promotion, corporate gifts, fund-raising, or educational purposes. Special editions can also be created to specifications. For details, contact the Special Sales Department, Sports Publishing, 307 West 36th Street, 11th Floor, New York, NY 10018 or sportspubbooks@skyhorsepublishing.com.

Sports Publishing® is a registered trademark of Skyhorse Publishing, Inc.®, a Delaware corporation.

Visit our website at www.sportspubbooks.com.

10 9 8 7 6 5 4 3 2 1

Library of Congress Cataloging-in-Publication Data is available on file.

Jacket design by Brian Peterson
Jacket photos from AP Images

Print ISBN: 978-1-61321-709-2
Ebook ISBN: 978-1-61321-730-6

Printed in the United States of America

CONTENTS

Section Five: Legacy

INTRODUCTION

THE OLDEST INDIVIDUAL I interviewed for this book was legendary coach and ESPN analyst Hubie Brown, who was eighty years old when I spoke to him at the 2014 NBA Finals. About Jordan, Brown said, "What he accomplished in his time, I don't think it's something you can match or that will be matched for a long time."

The youngest in these pages? Jabari Parker, the No. 2 pick in the 2014 NBA Draft, who was nineteen when he discussed being a Chicagoan experiencing the thrill of signing a contract with Brand Jordan shoes. When I asked Parker about the guy whose talents led to the shoe brand he would be wearing, Parker was careful to refer to him as "Mr. Jordan."

Brown was fifty-one years old when he first coached against Jordan, a 121–106 Bulls win in Madison Square Garden, which saw Jordan tally 33 points. Parker was born in 1995, just three days before Jordan issued his famous press release following his retirement from basketball and his brief baseball career, the one that said only: "I'm back."

The fact that both Brown and Parker—men of such different generations—perked up when I mentioned Jordan brought home just how resounding an impact he has had on basketball over the last three-plus decades. That an octogenarian coach and a teenage phenom could both somehow have a connection to one player seems almost unfathomable, but such is the wide net cast by Jordan. His was a career that can't be measured only in terms of excellence, but also in duration and lasting influence.

As a reporter covering the NBA, one of the frequent complaints you hear is that Jordan is difficult to know—even during his playing days, he was notably guarded and reluctant to reveal too much of his personality during interviews. He was master of the canned answer, meticulous in the way he presented himself. Once he finally hung up his high tops and retired (for good, in 2003), he became increasingly comfortable with an out-of-the-limelight role, reluctant to give interviews even as he was running the Wizards and, eventually, becoming owner of what is now the Charlotte Hornets.

Even in his relative reclusiveness, Jordan does offer up a legacy that speaks volumes, one that can be looked at in two ways. First, there are the accomplishments we've all seen, those moments of greatness etched into the collective sports memory. The 1987 and 1988 Slam-Dunk Contest championships, which elevated Jordan from young star player to Nike poster icon. "The Shot" that came against Cleveland to upset the Cavaliers on their home floor in 1989, forever immortalizing the frustration of Craig Ehlo. The hand-switch layup against the Lakers in the first game of the 1991 NBA Finals, Jordan's first appearance on the league's championship stage. The barrage of 3-pointers against the Blazers in 1992, knocking down so many that all he could do was look at the broadcast table and shrug. The free-throw line shot to sink the Jazz in Game 6 of the 1998 Finals, the championship-winning final act in his Bulls career (and one that Utahans still insist came as a result of an illegal push-off).

Those are plays we know, and they recur regularly with the help of years of highlight film replays and sports-drink ads. Then there is the other side of Jordan's legacy, which comes from those who were present at the time of those iconic plays. It is from those perspectives that you get a different look at vintage Jordan performances you might think you know so well, and those perspectives help to better put those plays in context.

You may remember Jordan's Slam-Dunk championship in 1987, but you probably don't know that the runner-up was actually a late fill-in for the injured Dominique Wilkins—and that the fill-in thought Terrence Stansbury should have been in the finals against Jordan.

You may remember "The Shot" against the Cavs, but you probably don't remember that Jordan missed a potential game-winning baseline jumper the game before and almost never shot from the baseline in a game-deciding situation again. You may remember Jordan dueling against Gary Payton in the 1996 NBA Finals, but you probably don't remember that the Sonics were hamstrung in that series by a back injury that limited guard Nate McMillan, who would have been guarding Jordan otherwise.

That is one goal of the stories that are included in this book—to give context, depth, and different viewpoints to the familiar moments of Jordan's career.

But beyond that, the goal is to bring to light the different parts of Jordan's time in basketball and the personality that most did not get to see. Jordan was a unique competitor, and the narratives included here highlight the intensity Jordan brought to the floor going all the way back to his days as a teenager playing pickup games, through his take-no-prisoners approach to practices and scrimmages when playing for Team USA in the early 1980s, to the mental and physical labor it took to lift himself past the Detroit Pistons in the late '80s and transform himself into the dominant force he became in the '90s.

Jordan has been portrayed as notably hardheaded and stubborn, for example. But for assistant coach Jim Cleamons, who worked with Jordan as part of Phil Jackson's staff, that was just not the Jordan he experienced. "As a teacher—and if you are a coach, you are a teacher first—you respected Michael because he allowed you to do your job," Cleamons told me. "That tells you a lot about the person."

And if Jordan was as self-interested as he is so often said to be, why did he take such an interest in extending a helping hand to Jay Williams, the Duke (egads, a Duke guy!) star drafted by Jordan's Bulls in 2002, even after Williams got into a motorcycle accident that ended his playing career? "He would talk to me all the time, encourage me to keep coming back, to keep fighting, to keep pushing," Williams said. "Spending time with that guy was really eye-opening."

Of course, no telling of Jordan's interaction with the rest of the basketball universe would be complete without delving into the way he turned the trash talk of lesser foes into fuel for masterpiece performances, finding new ways to drive his focus night after night. Even the most die-hard NBA fans are unlikely to remember short-termers like Willie Burton or Darrick Martin. But for Jordan, they were the kind of players who stepped a little too far over the line when it came to chatter—and whose team felt the sting of an on-court Jordan assault as a result.

As guard Byron Scott—who had to defend Jordan—once told Martin, when both were with Vancouver: "Hey, man, do me a favor. Don't talk [expletive] to my guy."

This is the nature of Jordan's career. Everyone around the game—players and coaches of all ages, it seems—has a Jordan anecdote of some sort; an instant in which their basketball lives intersected with his—in small ways or large—and in ways that were humorous or enlightening or even touching.

Jordan's numbers are easy to look up, as his highlights are readily available online. But these stories, I hope, offer a different, deeper, and more entertaining viewpoint than that with which most fans are already familiar.

Sean Deveney

Section One: Early Days

"A reporter from the *LA Times* was there and he asked
me about Jordan. And . . . I told him what I thought was
the truth. I said, 'I think Michael Jordan has a chance to go down as
the best basketball player to ever play the game.'"

—1984 Team USA assistant coach George Raveling

WE'VE ALL HEARD the legend—that Michael Jordan, playing for Laney High in Wilmington, North Carolina, was cut from his high school team as a sophomore and used the slight to fuel his hard work the following year, which led to him coming back to dominate as a junior. It makes for a nice script, but it is not exactly true. In fact, according to a story in the *Charlotte Observer*, Jordan was simply assigned to junior varsity, as nearly all the ninth- and tenth-graders of his era were. And when he was brought to the varsity, he was one of the best players in the state, reportedly averaging 29.2 points, 11.6 rebounds, and 10.1 assists as a senior.

Another myth: that Jordan was mostly held down during his three seasons playing for Coach Dean Smith at North Carolina and that no one really knew he would be an All-Star player until he came to the NBA. While Smith's Tar Heels were packed with talent in Jordan's time, he was a star in college, averaging 20.0 points as a sophomore and 19.6 as a junior, and winning the Naismith Player of the Year award in 1984. Throughout his junior season, many NBA executives who scouted him were considering him to be worthy of the No. 1 pick in the 1984 draft.

But it is true that when Jordan left college to enter the NBA, the most impressive and dominant basketball he had played came in the pickup

1

games he played in North Carolina and in the scrimmages that preceded the tournaments in which he participated for Team USA—the 1983 Pan-American Games, and the 1984 Olympics. In those games, he routinely embarrassed foes and dropped jaws in a way that he had not done in front of the television cameras in college.

In this section, we explore some glimpses at Jordan's early years, from those who guarded him in his college days, those who played with him in the early '80s international tournaments, those who witnessed his first years on the scene as a budding star in Chicago—and even from one player who Jordan has credited with inspiring his future excellence.

Walter Davis

Guard

College Career: North Carolina 1973–77
College Highlights: .... Won 1977 National Championship
NBA Career: 1978–1992
Career Highlights: .... 1978 NBA Rookie of the Year, six-time
All-Star

| Michael Jordan vs. Walter Davis | | | | | | | | | | |
Regular Season	Games	Wins	Losses	Win %	Field Goal %	PPG	Points (High)	RPG	APG	SPG
Jordan	12	9	3	75.0	56.2	37.8	52 (11/26/88)	7.3	7.8	2.2
Davis	12	3	9	25.0	40.7	16.9	31 (12/5/86	2.7	3.6	0.6

When Jordan was asked, in a 1997 interview, about his favorite players as he was coming up in basketball, he did not hesitate to answer: Walter Davis and David Thompson. Davis, like Jordan a 6-6 perimeter player,

starred at North Carolina from 1973–77 and helped the Tar Heels to the national championship game in 1977, where they lost to Marquette, 67–59. He went on to play 15 NBA seasons, earning six All-Star berths.

I MET MICHAEL JORDAN when he was just coming in to North Carolina. He had just come to school and had not played yet, it was still summer—maybe early September. All the pro guys would go back to North Carolina for a little while before we would go off to training camp. That was just a tradition we had. We would go there and play

3

each other and get into shape, and play against the kids who were on the team, the kids against the pros. Every afternoon at three o'clock, we would be out there playing, and we would play for hours, a couple hours at a time.

Michael was a freshman, and he was playing with us. Phil Ford—I had played with Phil at Carolina, and he had been playing for the Kings—Phil and I were playing on the same team, and we were trying to guard Michael. We couldn't catch him, he was so quick. He had one play where he beat both of us and went in and dunked the ball. I took it out of bounds and threw it in to Phil, we were walking up the court together and I said, "That kid is going to be pretty good." That was my first glimpse of Michael Jordan. He was seventeen years old then.

It is humbling to hear him say that I was an influence on him growing up, that he was a fan of mine. But that is one of the things about the game of basketball, the way it gets passed on from one group to the next and how each generation influences the next. I got tips from my brothers, from their friends—those guys helped me along the way. So I just tried to return the favor when I went back to Carolina. I showed Michael a couple of moves. I always thought it was important to help the younger players.

I worked with him on the jab-step and the pump-fake, which were some of my favorite moves. The midrange shot was something I emphasized, I remember telling him that was important to make that midrange shot. When he helped us win the [National] Championship in 1982, that shot was a midrange shot. I am not going to take credit for him making that, but I did try to tell him that the midrange shot was important. He had a lot of natural ability with that shot, he had good form on it, it looked good, everything. But he just needed to work on it so he could make it consistently.

What stood out to me was that Michael listened to instruction, he wanted to get better. If you told him something, he was going to work on it. We would be out there playing pickup games for two hours, and after we were done, we would go in the locker room, get dressed, shower, everybody had to ice their knees—that would take us an hour. We would finally get dressed, showered, and ready to go to dinner, and Michael would still be out there, practicing. He would be there doing that little spin off the glass that he was so good at when he would penetrate. He was still practicing that an hour after we had been playing for two hours, if you can imagine that. We were all going to dinner. I am not sure when he ate; all he seemed to do was work on his game.

Like I said, I knew he was going to be good when he was in college, you could see it in those pickup games. But when I finally got an idea just how good he would be, that was after his rookie year in the NBA. He came on the scene and you could see that his game was tailor-made for the league. Michael was so good fundamentally; I think that is something he got from playing for Dean Smith at North Carolina. I had already seen his work ethic, too, how much he was willing to put in every day to make himself a great player. When you combine that with his natural gifts—his talent and athletic ability—he is the total package. You can't help from being the best player in the league when you have all that on your side.

Michael got up for everybody. He always wanted to prove how good he was, he wanted to win the game, every time he stepped on the floor, that was all that was on his mind. That is something rare to see in a player with that much natural ability, that he was so competitive in everything, too. You have to remember, in those days, all the best players were the ones out on the wings. There were great big men and great point guards, but the stars of the league were the guys like Michael Jordan and Dominique Wilkins and Clyde Drexler, players like that. Every night there was going to be a challenge for you to guard, for you to go up against. I think that was something that drove Michael, too.

And I think there were times when he had extra motivation and that drove him in a way, made him reach down and be a little better. Against me, we had some good battles when we were both in the NBA. He had watched me in college and he liked my game, so naturally he wanted to try to beat me whenever we played. We would all still go back to Carolina in the off-season and have our pickup games, and you did not want to go back there and listen to all the other players talking about what they got against you in the regular season, in the NBA. So there was always something extra in those games.

I was in the Western Conference and he was in the East, so we did not get to play that often during the NBA season. The first time we played—he was not really a trash talker or anything—but he went out and he was terrific; he did everything and they won the game.[1] Two years after that, I was having a good year and we played twice, and those were both good battles, we went back and forth in those games. You always tried to make sure you were ready for those battles against him, because he was going to make a mental note and remind you about it in the pickup games.[2]

When I was a free agent in 1990, I was near the end of my career and was thinking about what I was going to do in retirement, what were some things that I might like to try. Michael called me up and tried to get me to come to the Bulls. He said I was someone who could help them win a championship—that was before they had won a title. Sometimes I think about that—one of my goals was to win an NBA championship and play in the NBA Finals—and Michael wanted to help me get one. Even now, when I see him, he reminds me that I could have had two rings if I had just signed on to play with them. But I knew once I finished playing with the Denver Nuggets, I would be working for them, as the front office had already asked me to do that. That was special for them to do that, to ask you to be a part of the organization. I had a family and they loved Colorado. I did broadcasting for six years for them after I retired, and that was something I don't regret.

---

[1] Jordan had 27 points, 14 assists, and nine rebounds in that game, on March 15, 1985.

[2] Jordan had 39 points to Davis's 27 on November 8, 1986, and had 43 points to Davis's 31 three weeks later (December 5). The Bulls and Suns split those two games.

But, certainly, winning those rings would have been nice, and it would have been great to play with him because I always enjoyed playing against him for all those years. For me, that was fun. Someone I had seen when he was so young and just coming up, to see him become the best player in the NBA—maybe the best player ever—and a Carolina guy. A good person, too, and that made it that much more fun.

Kenny "The Jet" Smith, who was Jordan's teammate at UNC, had a few words to add about his memory of him in college:

You could see the effort he was going to put into it [the game], but when he was at North Carolina, he wasn't a great basketball player; he was a great athlete playing basketball. He was not a good ball handler, and he didn't have a consistent shot from outside. But he was an incredible athlete. Once he got to the league, he worked on those skills that needed improvement and especially in terms of his shot, he got so much better. He didn't have to crash through the lane to score all the time. He could hit pull-up jumpers, and he really created the turnaround jumper for himself. But he was definitely a great athlete.

David Henderson

Guard

College Career: Duke University..................................1983–86
NBA Career: 1988

Henderson spent the bulk of his professional career overseas, but from 1983–86 he was an integral part of the team that helped turn around the Duke program—including a seminal win over North Carolina in the 1984 ACC Tournament in which Henderson had to defend Jordan.

OBVIOUSLY, MICHAEL WAS one of the most talented athletes in the country at North Carolina. He had a terrific freshman year and they won the [National] Championship in 1982.

I got to Duke the next year, I was a freshman and he was a sophomore. It was (and still is) a big rivalry, Duke-Carolina. But at that time, we were not as good, it was not the really big rivalry it has become now in the last twenty or thirty years. You knew right away he was a talented player, very difficult to defend, super-quick, and a big-time athlete. He wasn't a great ball handler then, but he was really, still, very skilled. Guarding him, you had to be alert all the time. The way Carolina played, they ran that backdoor play and he would kill you on that if you let him. He was one of the best at luring you to kind of lean out on him on the wing and then going back door, catching lobs and dunking, making the highlight film plays. He was very quick, so if you let him lull you to sleep, he was going to explode to the rim and you were not going to catch him.

He was a fierce competitor. What I learned most about him was what he was like in the off-season, actually, not so much during the NCAA season. At North Carolina, they had a structure to their system, and he fit into that. He was obviously great, but they played as a team so he was not as great individually. But in the off-season, going up against him in pickup games, that's when you saw the real Michael Jordan, the guy who would become Air Jordan, the guy everybody now knows. We would play pickup games in the area all the time: guys from Carolina, guys from Duke, whoever was around. He was a different player in those games. In that North Carolina system he was just a player, but in a pickup game he was tremendous. His will to win was there, he was driven. And these were just pickup games.

I remember one time, there was a pickup game, we were on the same team and we lost. The way it worked was, you lose, you have to sit and wait until it is your team's turn to play again. I remember we sat and waited, and he did not say anything. But when we went back on the floor for the next game, our team had the ball, it went over to him, and he drove in and scored. Next time down, ball goes to him, he scores. Next time, he scores. He scored 10 straight points in that game, and we won. I mean, you just knew the guy was special. If he would lose, it really drove him even more.

When we were playing Carolina, I was an ultracompetitive guy in general. That is kind of the way it was with me. Everything I did, I competed hard. I came to Duke and it was a perfect situation for me because I often felt like I was an underdog; I was not a top-level recruit or anything like that, and at Duke we were all taking on the challenge of reviving that program and becoming something special. [Coach Mike Krzyzewski] had just taken the job a couple of years earlier and knew what kind of players he wanted and how he wanted us to play. He thought we could be a power in the ACC. That was something that Coach K had recruited us all on. For me, I was a natural leader and when we played, winning mattered to me. I wasn't going to take losing. Toughness and all those things . . . that was what I tried to be about.

Being from North Carolina myself, I understood the ACC and I understood that North Carolina was at the top. If you wanted to get anywhere, you were going to have to go through UNC. It seemed like it had always just been that way. Being at Duke, that made me want to beat them all that much more, because I knew what the history there was, that it seemed like Carolina always had a leg up on everybody else. They certainly always seemed to have Duke's number.

We played them in the ACC Tournament in 1984, and that was a huge game, because we were going up against a really talented Carolina team. It was not just Michael Jordan, it was Kenny Smith and Brad Daugherty and Sam Perkins; they were like an All-Star team. They had lost only one game all year. We were the underdogs, obviously, because we were a young team that hadn't accomplished anything. The year before, in fact, we had lost to Virginia in that tournament; we lost that game by 40 points.[3] We were all freshmen at the time—me and Johnny Dawkins, Mark Alarie, Jay Bilas. It was the worst beating any of us ever had. So we vowed that would never happen again. That's why playing against Carolina in that tournament was so important to us.

We almost upset them twice during the regular season, but they were able to rally and pull out the win both times. The last time we had played them, it was only about a week before the ACC Tournament in the last game of the year, and I fouled out in that game. I had to guard Michael Jordan, and I played fourteen minutes and fouled out. That was frustrating for me, you can imagine. Jordan had 25 points against us, and they beat us in double overtime. We played them tough in both games, but ultimately came up empty.

So, I knew I would have to guard Jordan a lot in that ACC Tournament game. I knew I did not want that to foul out again.

---

[3] They had actually lost by 43 points, 109–66.

What was difficult about playing against him was that he was quick, but he could also post you up because he was so wiry strong. He was not bulky or anything, but he was very wiry and could get good position. What you have to do against a player like that is be a moving target, don't let him get in a comfort zone where it is just him posting you up. When a guy is passing it into the post to him, if you are moving and not giving him consistent contact, you can go wherever you want and it gives you the chance to get a jump on the pass and maybe poke it away, get out in transition. That's what I focused on.

In that game, I remember, it was back-and-forth. I remember Johnny Dawkins was tremendous, he threw some great passes—he was very good at throwing the lob—I remember catching some and finishing from him.[4] Jordan was Jordan in that game, he scored 20-plus points. But we did what we could to limit him. And there was a big play, late in the game, where Jordan was posting up on me and the pass came in to him, and it was sort of a high pass so I had time to reach over his shoulder to get to the ball. I was able to tap it away and set up the fast-break. I did bump him a little, and obviously I had remembered fouling out before. As soon as the play happened, I could hear Coach [Dean] Smith yelling at the refs, and I put my hands up because I thought they called a foul. I mean, they were Carolina so you always felt like they were going to get the calls. But there was no whistle, and we went down and scored. That helped turn the momentum to us.

It was tough. Michael Jordan was so good, and that team was so good. But we put it all together in that game and were able to win. That is when we knew we were starting to build something at Duke. Unfortunately, it took so much for us to beat them that Maryland came back the next day and knocked us off and won the tournament, but that was really the start of it [all]. That was when we started to feel like Duke basketball belonged at the top, when we beat Carolina and Michael Jordan in that tournament. It took off from there.

---

[4] Dawkins had 16 points and a game-high seven assists.

Dan Dakich

College Career: Indiana University 1981–85

Despite losing in the 1984 ACC Tournament, North Carolina was still a heavy favorite to win the National Championship, with only two losses on its record. But that was only until the Tar Heels ran into the Hoosiers in the Sweet 16, where Dakich—who averaged 3.9 points per game that year—was given the assignment of defending Jordan.

IT IS HARD to say exactly why we were able to win that one [the 1984 Sweet 16 matchup between Indiana and North Carolina] and what happened with me guarding Michael. Let me put it to you this

way: I was surprised after the game to hear that I had shut him down. I just thought we played a game and won. Then I went back to the hotel after the game and people were saying I shut him down, I thought *Okay, that's cool.* I always say, what the hell, if people want to think that, I am all for it. I just hope no one ever really watches the tape and sees what really happened. And if that is the case, then sure, I am cool with it.

The legend out there is that during our team meeting the day of the game, Coach [Bobby] Knight told me I was going to guard Michael Jordan that night, and I threw up. That is true, but it is out of context—I was sick the whole week, I had been throwing up for a week. But I wanted to play so I did not want Coach Knight or anybody to know I was sick, because he would put somebody else in. Somewhere along the way it got into Wikipedia or something that I threw up because I was guarding Michael Jordan. But that's not true. I was not scared or anything.

It was a Thursday night, the Sweet 16, in Atlanta. The way it worked was, we would have a meal three-and-a-half hours before all of our games. For a seven o'clock game, we would usually eat at 3:30. Then, after that, we would clear all the food and stuff away and Coach Knight would come in and would tell you the game plan. He would go over the starting lineups—with that team we had, we did not really know. We knew Steve Alford would start and we knew Uwe Blab would start. But that year, we had a lot of role players and the lineups were all kind of interchangeable and based on matchups. We would change lineups a lot. I thought I would start, but I wasn't quite sure.

Coach Knight is rattling off for us who is going to start and who's guarding who. He goes through: Steve Alford has Kenny Smith, Uwe Blab has Brad Daugherty, Mike [Giomi] on Sam Perkins, Marty Simmons taking Matt Doherty. And I was the last one. He looks and he says, "Dakich, you have Michael Jordan." And he said it like it was the last thing in the world he wanted to say, like all the greats who have been through Indiana—Isiah Thomas, Scott May, guys like that—and here we are playing North Carolina with Michael Jordan. And he has to put me on Jordan. I always thought he was disgusted just saying it, "Dakich, you have Michael Jordan." But it was me.

When you played there, you were supposed to know the book on everybody, not just on the guy you were guarding. Big guy, small guy, it did not matter; you were just supposed to know. That was the way we went about it. So we went over all of that.

For Jordan it was: play off of him, because you want to make him shoot jump shots. The way it worked was, an assistant coach would go over the scouting report and he would go over it in depth, whatever the characteristics were about the individual and the team. During practice, we would go over the scouting reports. But on the day of the game, Coach Knight would give three or four things to have in your mind, so your brain is not cluttered. Knight, to me, said three things I could *not* do: Do *not* let him post you up. Do *not* let him offensive rebound. Do *not* let him back-cut. He said, "If you do any one of those things, I will take you out." I thought, *Okay, I could do that.*

Pregame meal at Indiana was a combination of spaghetti, hamburgers, scrambled eggs, and ice cream. Things like that. I was so stupid, I thought I was sick, so I would just eat my way through it. You don't feel good, so you eat to make yourself feel better. That is how dumb I was. I ate. I ate a lot. I took the elevator up and I remember, I threw up between the room and the door, there was a little entryway. A little in the room, a little outside the room. But that was because I was sick as a dog. I threw up the day before. I would have thrown up no matter who I was guarding.

When we got to the arena—it was the Omni, in Atlanta—it was just an electric atmosphere. It was Indiana-Carolina, those are two teams that were the best known programs in the country. They were stacked, they had NBA players all over the lineup, you know, not just Jordan. We had read an article where some guy was saying that Carolina was the greatest team in the history of NCAA basketball. Ever. Coach Knight showed us that. But we were Indiana. We had beaten Carolina in 1981 for the title, which was a win a lot of people remembered. We were a great program ourselves. That Carolina team was No. 1 in the nation, but Indiana had a long history of winning games like that, so our fans were expecting us to win.

And Coach Knight had us expecting that we *could* win. What he did was—I will never forget this because I used it when I was coaching, too—he came in that Sunday when we were back on campus, four days before the game. We played Saturday, we beat Richmond to get to the Sweet 16. We then we flew home the night after the game and had a six or seven o'clock meeting that night. I will never forget, he came into the meeting room and he said, "Okay, we are going to beat North Carolina's ass. And if anyone doesn't think we are going to beat North Carolina's ass, they can get the [expletive] out of this room right now. That is not just the players. That includes you, coaches. That includes you, managers. That includes you, trainers. Because I am going to close this door and if you don't think we are going to beat their ass, get the [expletive] out of the room."

No one left, so he closed the door and said, "Okay, now let me tell you how we are going to do it." I always thought that was a great way to approach it, and I used that myself in my own coaching career.

Finally, when the game started, first minute of the game, I am guarding Jordan and he scores twice. Bam, bam. My reaction was, *Great, he is going to get 160 points.* I swear to God, I was coming down the court and—my brain just works this way—I was looking up at the façade where the scoreboard was and the score's 4–0, North Carolina, and Jordan had all four. I am running down the floor and I see that and I do some quick math, four points, there are forty minutes. I said to myself, *[Expletive], he is going to score 160 points in this game.*

But truthfully, you could kind of tell that Carolina kind of thought they were all equals. That was how they played. When Kenny Smith had a shot, he was going to take it. Matt Doherty was going to shoot. Like they were taking turns. They had Sam Perkins and Michael Jordan on the team, and I was out there thinking, *Damn, throw the ball to Perkins or throw the ball to Jordan and stop shooting.* But they just kept doing this equal-opportunity thing. That was their deal. For us, our deal was get the ball to Steve Alford, as he is going to make his shots. I remember Buzz Peterson came in off their bench, he jacked up a jump shot from the corner. Kenny Smith had a bad wrist, but he was still shooting. Steve Hale was taking shots. And I thought, *Hey, this is okay with us.*

Our game plan was mostly just to be tougher than them. Because I don't think Coach Knight had a lot of respect for that roster in a grind-it-out kind of game. He knew how good they were, he knew how good Jordan was, but his attitude was: we are going to fight you on screens, we are going to push you around where we can. We did not feel like they were that mentally tough.

And really, you had guys on their team asking out of the game and things like that. We were different. I was sick all game and still trying to guard Michael Jordan. During the game, on the bench, there was a big old security guard, I asked him to bring me a bucket. I took a towel and put it over my head, because there is no dignity in throwing up on national TV—I did not think so, anyway. So I put a towel over me, over my head. I puked right into the bucket.

Michael got into some foul trouble, he had two fouls eight minutes or so into the game. And they took him out. To be honest, I never understood why they kept him out so long. It wasn't like they were a defensive team, it wasn't like they were some scrappy team that needed to play really tight D to win. They trapped—they did things like that—but they didn't need to have him playing right up on everyone. Leave him in there, tell him to be careful. But he got two fouls and sat down right there. Then after that, they were bringing him in and out, in and out. They would bring him in for a possession or two, then they would take him out, that kind of thing. That was great for us—hell, keep him out. He could not get a real rhythm.

I wound up fouling out. The last foul—I did not think was a foul at all—I opened up on a back screen and if they threw it up in the air, Jordan was going to dunk it. But they threw it low and I got a piece of the ball and they called a foul on me. It was one of those deals where, I was tired, I reached. I didn't touch him, but I could see why the ref would call it. But I still tell my teammates—even now—I held the guy to nine [points] and those guys gave up four to him after I fouled out, in the last couple of minutes.[5] I am never close to being serious about that, just to be clear. It's pretty funny.

I hear it all the time from Carolina people who try to sort of do revisionist history on the whole thing. They tell me, "Well, Kenny Smith was hurt, he hurt his wrist." And I always tell them, Coach Knight always told us Winston Morgan was our best player—Winston Morgan was hurt at that time. He wasn't really our best player, Alford was, but that is just one of the things Coach Knight liked to do to motivate us. People say Kenny Smith was hurt, I come back and say, "Winston Morgan didn't even play."

We won the game, Alford was great down the stretch and we pulled it off. It was big. We just beat the No. 1 team in the country, supposedly the greatest college team ever, on a big night. But we were a ridiculous team. We would beat really good teams, then turn around and lose to Miami of Ohio. We were kind of a front-running team, so we were really happy with beating Carolina. But we were exhausted. We were excited, but I got back to the locker room and I was throwing up again, I was dehydrated. It was the No. 1 team in the country, we were excited, but it was also like, we're Indiana, we're supposed to beat teams like that. If we were Cleveland State, that would be a different story.

I am sure Michael is frustrated by it to this day; they were a great team. But screw him. I am still frustrated by the fact that we lost the next game to Virginia. We should have beaten them. I am haunted by that.[6] You don't have to be a great player to be haunted by a loss, you don't have to be the greatest player ever.

I did hang out with him later, after that game. It was during the Team USA trials that they held at Indiana a few months later, they were getting ready for the Olympics and picking that team. We played golf, and I got him for $6,000. True story. It was me, him, Steve Alford, and

---

[5] Jordan averaged 19.6 points per game during the 1984 season.
[6] Indiana lost in the 1984 Elite Eight to Virginia, 50–48.

Timmy Knight, Coach Knight's son. I was really good back then. I had just played 18 holes, I was hitting balls afterward, and those three come up. I played with them till it got dark.

After the first couple of holes, Jordan got frustrated, so he kept raising the bets, kept making them double or nothing. He was really bad back then, he was just learning to play and by the end, it was $6,000. And he never paid me. The next day, they were at their practice and I was there, just watching. I saw him and was like, "Hey, about that six grand . . ." and he is trying to give me like plain-pocket jeans they got for being part of the Team USA thing. Levi's was a sponsor, and he was trying to give me those jeans and a Polaroid camera. I was like, "Dude, you owe me six grand." He never paid me. To this day. That is his reputation, I guess. Too bad, I could have used six grand.

George Raveling

Raveling enjoyed a long relationship with Jordan, serving as an executive at Nike, but that relationship was founded during the 1984 USA Basketball tryouts at Indiana—Raveling, the head coach at Iowa, was an assistant to Bob Knight with that team—and the Americans' run to that year's gold medal.

IN MY MIND, those 1984 Olympic trials were one of the greatest displays of competitive basketball we are ever going to see, and nobody really stood out at that time quite the way Michael Jordan did.

You had Chris Mullin, Patrick Ewing, Charles Barkley, Karl Malone, just so many very talented players who were involved. This was probably the ultimate competitive stage that they could be on and exhibit the enormous skills that they had. It was so competitive that an NBA scout sitting there watching could watch what these players were doing and transfer it in his mind to the court. A lot of them were there doing that.

We started in Bloomington, Indiana, where Coach [Bobby Knight] was. It was packed, he had so many players and everything had to be run just right. There was so much talent out there, and they were under intense pressure just to make the team. They were fighting each other for those spots, for weeks and months. We started in Bloomington, and then traveled all around the country playing exhibition games against NBA players. It was a very big challenge.

But over the course of all that time, it became obvious just how good Michael was. When we finally got up to the Olympic village at the end of July, a reporter from the *LA Times* was there and asked me about Jordan. And Coach Knight was not too happy that I was quoted as saying this, but I told him what I thought was the truth. I said, "I think Michael Jordan has a chance to go down as the best basketball player to ever play the game."

That was based entirely on what I saw during those trials. I knew Michael was good before the trials; I was coaching at Iowa, and I knew about him at North Carolina. He was a very good player there. They had won the National Championship when he was a freshman. But he was far better than I ever realized he was once he got to those trials.

He did things at practice that I have never seen a human being do on a basketball court, with his athleticism and his ability to hang in the air. And I think that the more I saw, the more it was obvious that he defined the phrase, *elite talent.* Because his game was multi dimensional, he could do so many things on an extraordinary level. Not good, not adequate, not even great—extraordinary. Yet, he was a team player. He would play defense, he would pass, he would do all the things you want to see your star do. He was a regular, down-to-earth person.

Michael and I became lifelong friends as a result of 1984—Michael, Patrick Ewing, myself, and Vern Fleming. We became inseparable at the trials and all during the Olympics. We would go shopping together, sightseeing together, we would go out to eat together. When you are together for that long in that kind of environment, you are going to form close bonds.

The day of the 1984 draft—it was actually a Tuesday—and we were still in Indiana for the trials. The draft was not on one of the big television stations, it was not as big as it is now. The players were not allowed to leave the camp to go to the draft in New York. So I took them to a TV station in Bloomington, and they remoted it back to New York.

There had been a lot of talk about where everyone was going to go, about Houston liking [Hakeem] Olajuwon and Portland going for [Sam] Bowie. But it wasn't quite like it is now with the mock drafts and all of that. I still thought Michael was the best player and should have gone No. 1. He did not know he was going to go No. 3. He thought he still might go No. 1, even though Olajuwon was there. Or to Portland with the No. 2 pick. So it was kind of shocking when he went No. 3, at least to us.

My biggest concern was the team he played for—was he going to somewhere where they would allow him to be whom he could be? He was picked by Chicago, and you could only hope that the Bulls had that plan for him, which they eventually did. The great coaches provide an environment where the player can reach his outer limits. He can discover his own greatness. A guy like Jordan, you can't put fences around him. The style of play sometimes limits the player's ability. Greatness, you have to liberate the greatness. There has to be an environment that allows greatness to manifest itself.

That's why I always laugh when people talk about Coach [Dean] Smith being the only guy to hold Michael under 20 points or whatever it is they say. Coach Smith did just what he should have done in developing Michael. The job is not to prove to America that Michael Jordan is the best player. It is up to people to figure that out for themselves on their own. His responsibility was to win the ACC and compete for the National Championship, and if within that system Michael exhibits his abilities, then fine. But it has to happen within the system, and Michael understood that at the time. They won. He had to sacrifice, but it was for the best. That's an important lesson for a young player, one that maybe not enough players learn now.

After the draft was over—it was in the afternoon then—we only had an hour and twenty minutes till we had to be back at practice. So I told the guys we had to hustle, they had to get taped and all that. I asked, "What do you want to eat?"

And Michael, before anybody could say anything, said, "McDonald's."

I said, "McDonald's? Man, you are a millionaire now. You cannot go eating McDonald's."

He said, "Coach, I don't care how much money I make, I am a McDonald's guy." So, the first thing Michael Jordan did after he got drafted was go to McDonald's.

Obviously, Michael developed into the greatest player of all-time, and I think you could see that he would eventually be something close to that when you watched him in those trials. But what I did not see at that time was just how much drive he had, how much drive he had to win and be the best. You can't necessarily tell that until someone's career gets going.

That's the thing about Michael. I have been around him a lot; I have run his basketball camp for nineteen years. I have not met anybody who is as competitive with everything as Michael is—any facet of life. I mean, he just wants to win all the time. It's nothing bad, he just takes it seriously.

There is a part of his camp when he gives an offensive lecture, then takes kids out and plays them one-on-one. And if they beat him, they get a year supply of Jordan stuff. One year, he is out there, and a kid had him down, 2–0, a fourteen-year-old kid. From that time on, Michael played him like it was the NBA Finals, Game 7 or something.

After that, I am driving back with him to the hotel. I said to him, "Why didn't you let the kid win?"

And he said, "Coach, you're crazy as hell. I am not going out there to lose."

I said, "But he's only fourteen years old."

He said, "Coach, I am not letting him win so that he can go through life saying he beat Michael Jordan one-on-one."

That's Michael, though. It is his competitive nature that makes him so great.

Frank Burlison

In the days before year-round mock drafts, Burlison was a pioneer, working as both a reporter for Knight Ridder *and a recruiting scout who monitored some of the top young basketball talent in the nation, and was on hand for the 1984 USA Olympic trials and games. Burlison was a 2005 inductee in the USBWA Hall of Fame.*

IT WAS REALLY just an incredible thing to have all these players gathered in one spot, all trying to make this Olympic team, and then you had all these coaches there, all the NBA people, all the national writers. It was a unique thing, and you think about the players who made

the team, like Chris Mullin and Sam Perkins and Patrick Ewing. But then you think of the ones who got cut—John Stockton, Charles Barkley—and you get an idea of the level of talent. But it was clear at the time that the best player out there, the one who stood out the most, was Michael Jordan.

I remember the last day of camp—before the cuts—how much of a different era it was. At the time, the NBA Draft was sort of looming over the whole thing, and there were NBA personnel people there, they were watching it, they were talking to the coaches, they were talking to [Team USA Head Coach] Bobby

Knight. At the time, though, it was not sure whether Jordan was going to enter in the draft. He was a junior and I think most people thought he would, but they had lost in the NCAA Tournament just a few weeks before, in the regional finals, when [Dan] Dakich really held him down for Knight and Indiana. Carolina lost that game, and you could tell it bothered him.

Back then, there was not what you see today where there is so much hype and people talking about, "Is this guy going or not going?" It was not unusual for a player to go back for his senior season. There were no year-round mock drafts. So no one really knew what Jordan was going to do, stay or go. I just remember, everyone thought Jordan was the best player at the camp, but we did not know how good he would go on to be. You could tell he was going to have a good career—he was very athletic—but no one would have guessed he would be arguably the greatest player, you did not know he was going to be an icon. It was not like LeBron James being on the cover of *Sports Illustrated* when he was a teenager.[7]

I remember after the first day of practice—there was no formal interview process—you could just walk up and start talking to whoever you wanted. I will never forget, I just walked up to Michael and started talking with him, maybe five or six minutes, just him and me. So I told him, I had been hearing from NBA people that he was going to be one of the top picks if he came out and entered the draft. He said he really did not know what he was going to do, that he just did not want to think about that now. So for a while there, he was at least considering going back to Carolina, maybe to get over that loss they had to end the 1984 season.

But I look back on that and, what an innocent time, right? How many times have reporters just been able to walk up to Michael Jordan and start talking to him for a few minutes, alone?

---

[7] LeBron James made the cover of *Sports Illustrated* at age eighteen, while still in high school. Michael Jordan was twenty when he first made it onto the cover (with teammate Sam Perkins while at UNC).

Everyone knew Michael was a very good college player on what was a great college team, with Jordan and Worthy and Sam Perkins, Brad Daugherty. But he averaged 19 points or so,[8] and he was good, but he was just a part of the team in college. He had made the big shot when he was a freshman to win the tournament in 1982, but he had not had the same success since and I think a lot of the media bought into the BS that Dean Smith was the only guy who could hold Michael Jordan under 25 points a night, that kind of thing. A lot of people had the wrong idea about him.

Watching him at that time, though, it was clear that he just did things so easily and he was so well rounded. That was when you could begin to see that he might be a great, great player. You got the feeling he could do anything he wanted to. He could score at any time, he could be a playmaker, he could rebound if he wanted to, and that was what the team needed. Even though he was not sure about the draft, it seemed like the scouts and the NBA people who were watching were sure. During that time, it went from, "Okay, how good is he going to be at Carolina, how much is going to crush it for Dean Smith next year?" to "What is he going to be able to bring to an NBA team right away?" I didn't think he was going to be one of the best players of all-time. But I came away convinced he would be an All-NBA in the NBA for a long time.

Having said that, Jordan was obviously great, but it wasn't one of those deals where you just knew he was going to turn into what he eventually became. I would compare it to maybe hearing the Beatles for the first time, or seeing Robert DeNiro the first time in *Mean Streets*—you might think, *Wow, this sounds great* or *That guy is really good.* But you don't immediately think that, twenty-five years from now, you'll still be talking about him as an icon beyond the game itself.

---

[8] 19.6

Pat Williams

Williams's career in sports management is spread over five decades, and includes the founding of the Orlando Magic, which came into being in 1989, and for whom Williams still works. But in the 1980s, Williams built the NBA champion Sixers teams, and he spent most of the 1983–84 season certain his Sixers had a shot at the No. 1 pick—and had their sights set on a certain North Carolina guard.

MICHAEL JORDAN WAS part of that 1984 [NBA] Draft, and it was really just a historic draft. But at the time, we really did

not know just how historic it was going to be. We just knew it would be really, really good.

I remember it vividly. I was [the general manager] in Philadelphia, and we had been preparing for that draft all year. We were a good team then, we were coming off a championship in the 1983 season and had Moses Malone and Julius [Erving] and Maurice Cheeks, Andrew Toney. We were good again the next year. But we had made a trade—six years earlier— we sent Lloyd Free to San Diego for the Clippers' first-round pick in 1984,[9] both of us probably thinking that that day would never come. When you make a

---

[9] The Clippers played in San Diego from 1979–84.

trade like that, it's hard to imagine that, six years later, there is going to be a payoff.

But that day did come, and we had the pick belonging to the Clippers that year. Now, the Clippers were the Clippers as usual, and through the course of the season they were the worst team in the West. They were three or four games worse than anyone else for most of the year.[10] That was the cause of some excitement for us. Knowing that [Hakeem] Olajuwon was lurking there, and that Michael Jordan was lurking there, we knew the magnitude of that draft. No one knew just how great this class was going to be, but it was obvious there were some good players. And we were at the front of the line to get one of them.

At the time, the worst teams were sorted out by a coin flip between the two conferences. Portland had Indiana's pick, and the Pacers were the worst in the East. Throughout the whole year, we were in the coin flip for the West, as the Clippers were struggling. We were thinking Olajuwon, we were thinking Jordan. One of those guys was coming to Philadelphia, we thought.

That is, until Houston, the last month or so, went totally in the tank, losing nine of their last ten games. It was obvious. They had won the coin flip the year before and took Ralph Sampson, and they had visions of Ralph Sampson and Olajuwon. So they completely died, blatantly, really. On the last night of the season, we were still right there, we had a chance at being in the coin flip. But the Rockets lost, and darned if the Clippers don't win, they beat the Jazz and finish with 30 wins.[11] Houston wound up in the coin flip, and they get the No. 1 pick. On the last night of the year, we go from coin flip, Olajuwon or Jordan, to the fifth pick. In one night. We were devastated. Absolutely devastated.

But it is interesting to consider is, if things had gone right for us, if we would have been in that position, would we have gone with Olajuwon

---

[10] They would finish the season with a 30–52 record, which was the second-worst record in the West (only to the 29–53 Rockets).
[11] The Clippers beat the Jazz, the 2-seed in the West, 146–128.

or Jordan? Billy Cunningham was our coach at the time, and he was a North Carolina guy and a devoted Tar Heel. [North Carolina Coach] Dean Smith, of course, would always try to land his players with fellow Tar Heels when he could. North Carolina guys were always taking care of each other.

Nevertheless, we talked long and hard as that season was coming to an end about what we were going to do. We knew that Olajuwon was going to be a great center, and we were wary on Sam Bowie, the player that Portland wound up taking. But nobody quite knew what the upside on Jordan was going to be. The truth is, our scout told us about Jordan: "We could take him, and he could back up Julius [Erving] at forward and he could back up Andrew Toney on the guard line." So we thought he could play small forward and we thought he could play two-guard and that he would make a good backup for the players we had, Julius and Andrew.

Michael Jordan, a sixth man in Philadelphia. Turns out, he was a little better than that.

We are often asked what we would have done, and we spent a lot of time considering it. Keep in mind that, for the entire season, we were in the coin flip. I don't know exactly what we would have done, if we would have gone with Olajuwon or Jordan. I think at the end of the day, honestly, Dean Smith would have prevailed, because he would have campaigned intensely for Michael, and Billy Cunningham would have pushed for it. But you couldn't go wrong. You get a Hall of Fame center like Olajuwon, or you get the greatest player of all-time. But we never had to make that choice.

The draft comes and Houston goes with Olajuwon, Portland goes big and takes Sam Bowie. And there is Michael, hanging out for Chicago. [Bulls general manager] Rod Thorn made the call on that one. Dallas goes with Sam Perkins fourth. And we are sitting at No. 5, looking at a 6-4, 292-pound power forward. And as the late Jack McMahon described Charles Barkley, he was a ball-handling Westley Unseld. We take Sir Charles [from Auburn], not knowing quite what we had.

But as we look back, he ends up as one of the 50 best players of all-time[12] and maybe the most unique athlete ever to play any sport and a once-in-a-lifetime talent. We can't complain too much.

After that, I left Philadelphia, and we started up the team in Orlando. We had Michael staring us in the face for years, it seemed. The Bulls were the measuring stick for everyone. That was the case for the whole league, especially for the Eastern Conference. We got by them one time, in 1995, when he was coming back from having played baseball for two years. But that was it.

We could have had him in Philadelphia. In hindsight, he put the NBA on his back and carried the league for years and years, so I suppose it was all worth it.

---

[12] Also referred to as the NBA's 50th Anniversary All-Time Team, which was announced in 1996.

Ed Pinckney

Forward

Career: **1986–97**

Michael Jordan vs. Ed Pinckney										
Regular Season	Games	Wins	Losses	Win %	Field Goal %	PPG	Points (High)	RPG	APG	SPG
Jordan	20	13	7	65.0	55.7	36.3	49 (2/19/88)	6.6	5.0	2.9
Pinckney	20	7	13	35.0	58.7	7.0	19 (4/20/90)	4.7	0.9	0.9

Pinckney is best remembered for his collegiate exploits, leading Villanova to the 1985 National Championship and translating that into a 12-year NBA career. But before all of that, he participated in the 1983 Pan-American games in Venezuela, where he was a teammate of Jordan.

MICHAEL JORDAN AND I were in the same high school class, so I had an idea how good he was. I had played against him. But it wasn't until the Pan-American Games that I really saw how fast he had developed and how good he was.

We were in Caracas during that time. That was a great team, the late Wayman Tisdale was on that team, and Michael Cage, Chris Mullin, and Mark Price. We had a lot of fun, but what we learned in that time was just how good Michael Jordan was. We all—all of us—marveled at what he was able to do. On that trip, we played a collection of three professional teams at various stops around the country. We played against a lot of NBA players, and he was unreal during that whole time. We were all saying that we knew he was good, but he was a lot better than we even knew. We were just marveling after each game at how good he was.

I can remember on that team—Leon Wood was on that team. Leon was close with Michael at that time, and Leon was always saying, "Man, this is *the* guy." Leon was the point guard, so of course, he was smart enough to know that if there was any doubt, throw it to Michael. We were all pretty good players, all first-round picks and whatever, but he just, during that trip, Jordan separated himself. We all knew he was going to be a really special player.

Even during the tryouts, it was amazing to be part of that. There were about 100 of us trying out for that team, and they had us all divided up into groups, and we would scrimmage against each other. They had these games that would go to seven; first team to seven would win. When I was on his team, I don't think we lost. We would go out there and it would be 7–0, all seven points for Michael. There was no one who could stop him during those tryouts. They had just lost in the NCAAs, and you could tell he was mad and just wanted to get better and better. I remember looking at some of the guys on the team, the guys we were trying out with and saying, "It is out of control how good he has gotten."

What really stood out was just the tenacity that he had and the way he started to bring it every single play. He was in really good condition, he took that seriously. You saw that during that time, and nobody was playing that way during the training camps and in the scrimmages. But you would hear some of the guys who were playing on the pro teams, guys who were in the NBA. After playing against us for a few minutes, they were all saying, "Hey that kid is good." These were men, pros, who were saying that—we were still college kids at the time. So it was a privilege to sort of watch the early origins of him as a player.

He came out for the draft in 1984 after his junior year at North Carolina, and I stayed at Villanova for another year.[13] After that, I got drafted by the Suns with the 10th pick. When I was there, I played with Walter Davis as a rookie, and I can remember that when Chicago came to town, Walter would get especially focused around that time.

Walter was a great player in his own right. He was getting older but still scoring 20 points per game[14] and he had been around eight years, he was an All-Star multiple times.[15] Michael had been having a great first couple of years in the league and was obviously a great scorer. But Walter had extra focus when he knew Michael Jordan was coming in. I remember Larry Nance was on our team, and he said, "Hey, Walter, he is just a young kid, don't worry about it." They didn't have the NBA package at that time, so you could not necessarily watch other teams and you didn't really watch teams in the other conference. And I am sitting there listening to Larry Nance and saying, "This is no regular young kid. He is a little better than that."

But Walter already knew that because he had spent so much time with him at Carolina. They had a long relationship. Michael respected Walter, he would always talk about Walter's will to win, how he always kept himself in shape and top condition. And that was something Michael always took away from him, something that Walter taught him when Michael was still at Carolina. But that did not mean Michael didn't want to beat him. Walter knew it, and this was an eight- or nine-year vet talking about a second-year guy. But he knew when Michael was going to be playing against Phoenix. And he was like, "I have got to get ready for this guy."

---

[13] Pinckney led the eighth-seeded Wildcats to a shocking NCAA championship in 1985, defeating No. 1 Georgetown for the National Championship.

[14] Davis averaged 21.8 points that year, at age thirty-one.

[15] During his career, Davis was a six-time All-Star and the 1978 Rookie of the Year.

The Bulls came in and Chicago was on their way up at the time, but they were still a young team and trying to figure themselves out; they were not the team that was going to the playoffs and winning championships every year. Michael was still pretty much their only weapon, and he was really dominant individually. I can remember, the first couple of baskets he made in my first game against him, they were those reverse, off-the-glass shots he would make. I was in the game guarding the paint and I would go over to help and he would start on this side of the rim, so I would try to step in front of him. But then, he would be on the other side of the rim just like that. That's how athletic he was. And you're looking like, "How did he get over there?" He was doing those moves, and Walter is looking at Larry Nance as if to say, *You see what I mean? This is not a normal young guy.*

But it was a privilege to play with him in those early days, at the Pan-American Games, because that was when I really started seeing how special he was going to be down the line. You probably could not have predicted he was going to become everything he eventually was, but you could tell he was going to be a great, great NBA player.

Eddie Johnson

Guard/Forward

Career: 1982–99
Career Highlights: .... 1989 Sixth Man of the Year

Michael Jordan vs. Eddie Johnson										
Regular Season	Games	Wins	Losses	Win %	Field Goal %	PPG	Points (High)	RPG	APG	SPG
Jordan	24	19	5	79.2	50.2	34.0	53 (1/21/89)	6.5	5.6	2.4
Johnson	24	5	19	20.8	49.8	14.9	29 (twice)	3.3	1.8	0.2

Johnson is a 17-year NBA veteran, having played for six teams from 1981–99. He was part of the group of professionals that played against Jordan and Team USA in the scrimmages leading up to the 1984 Olympics before getting to know Jordan as an NBA star.

FOR ME, THERE is no story that stands out as much as this one with Michael. It was 1988, I was with Phoenix, I was a veteran, and Michael was now getting to be a veteran, too. We were traveling for the preseason, we had been in Louisville, I think, and then I believe we were in St. Louis. We were supposed to play them two games, and we had beaten them the first game, we blew them out. It was an exhibition, though, not a really big deal.

The way it worked then, you did not have a team plane carting you around. We were on the same plane after the game; we were staying in the same hotel, because it was just an exhibition. We won the game, so of course, we saw them afterwards and were talking. We saw them on the plane the next morning and were talking more junk on the plane. We got into the hotel, and in the morning they had some food for us. And we did not let up; we were talking junk down there, too. And I remember Michael talking junk back to us, but we had won the game. Tom Chambers and Ty Corbin and me, we were saying, "Yeah, we busted you all up last night."

So Michael says, "Well, let's see what happens tonight." Not a big deal, just an exhibition game.

But then he said, "First, let's go up to my room and we will play some cards." A lot of us in the league would play a game called Tonk, so we said, "Okay, fine," and we went up to play some Tonk for a while. I was thinking I would go in and play cards for two or three hours and then go and get some rest before the game; that is how we usually did it.

Well, lo and behold, we got to his room at about ten in the morning, Scottie Pippen was there, as was Jack Haley and Horace Grant. The bus for the game was at six. It got to be two or three o'clock, and I was thinking it was time to leave, get some rest, get ready for the game. We had had a tough training camp. Cotton Fitzsimmons, our coach, had really worked us hard. So a lot of us were sore. But Michael, he wouldn't let us leave the room. He wanted to keep playing. So we stayed in his room, playing cards, and it got to maybe about twenty or thirty minutes before the bus was going to leave.

At that time, I had been sitting playing cards all day, I stood up and my legs were almost numb. I was sore. We were in a small hotel room and so it was a little uncomfortable. I called Cotton and I said, "You know, Cotton, I am still sore from last night, I don't even want to play this exhibition game."

He said, "Don't worry, Eddie, I was not going to play you that much anyway."

Tom Chambers was there, too, and now he didn't want to play either. But I had beaten him to the punch. He gets on the phone, calls Cotton and says, "I am a little beat up; I don't know if I want to play." Cotton might have been getting a little suspicious, but he said, "Fine." Two of his best players, he was not going to risk them playing in the last exhibition.

Now, Ty Corbin wants to call, too, but he can't do it; not after me and Tom had just called. It would have been too obvious. So Ty is sitting there, like, "Thanks, guys." He had to play. So he left.

It was not long before the bus was supposed to leave and we were still in the room, still playing Tonk, and Michael looked at us and said, "I am going to give your boy 40 tonight." He was talking about Dan Majerle with the Olympics. He was in the Olympic trials with Michael in 1988 before the Olympics, and there was talk that Dan played good defense on Michael. Even [Bulls general manager] Jerry Krause was saying it. Michael was telling us, "People say he stopped me during the Olympic trials." He wanted to show that there wasn't anybody who was going to stop him, he told us that.

I was thinking, it's just an exhibition game. I got up from sitting there all day and I couldn't even walk—how is he going to think about giving somebody 40 in an exhibition game? Dan Majerle was a rookie on our team, and there was a story that Krause had tried to get him to stay out of some of the college exhibition games so the Bulls could draft him, and he had been telling Jordan how good Majerle would be.[16]

Michael went out, and I mean, he lit it up. Cotton put Dan Majerle on him, and just he lit Dan up. Right from the beginning. Michael scored something like 25 points in the first quarter. He was talking to him, he was talking to us, he was talking to our bench, telling us what

---

[16] Krause had supposedly promised Majerle the Bulls would take him in the third round, but Majerle wound up being drafted 14th by the Suns. Jordan routinely liked to dress down Majerle because of the way Krause had talked him up.

move he was going to do. There was one point, he came over and said to Cotton, "I am going to take him to the baseline and dunk on him." Next play, he goes to the baseline and dunks on Dan. There was just nothing you were going to do to stop it.

It was hysterical. Tom Chambers and I kept looking at each other. We were not playing, so we could laugh about it. Ty Corbin was not happy, because he knew what was going on and he had to play. Cotton Fitzsimmons was there wondering what was going on. I mean, it was an exhibition! He had no idea why Michael was giving us the treatment like that. Cotton called a timeout and he grabbed Dan Majerle and asked him, "What did you to him? What did you say to him? Why did you get him so mad at us?"

And Dan was a very emotional guy, and just yells back, "I didn't do anything to him, Cotton! I swear!" Oh, we were laughing. Because we knew.

That was the beauty of Michael, though. Just a very competitive guy. The way he got to 40, it was unreal; the way he was flying and dunking and getting up and down the court—and this was an exhibition game! I was sitting on the bench, hardly able to move because I had sat so long.

That was at the point of his career where he was still figuring things out. I had seen him long before, at the Olympic trials in 1984, when he was just coming out of North Carolina. That team played an exhibition game against us in Kansas City. I played in that game. We were not that sure about the young guys who were in there, but we came out and you could see right away that offensively, Michael Jordan was special. He could do whatever he wanted. We were trying to play up and challenge him, but he would just jump right over you and embarrass you. Right away, we saw it.

When he came in, obviously, it was a situation where we all knew he could score. The league was bracing itself at that time, with Magic Johnson and the Lakers and Larry Bird and the Celtics. But with

Michael, I don't know that anyone really knew what the NBA had at that point. Him being in Chicago really helped. After the first two or three weeks, it was obvious he was an unbelievable scorer.

But guess what? We had already witnessed George Gervin, and I still think Gervin is the best pure scorer the league has ever seen. We had Dominique Wilkins, too, a guy who could just plain score anytime he wanted. But that is not enough to be a championship player. Michael showed us his scoring and elevating and flying through the air, adding a little bit more pizzazz to it—sort of like David Thompson, though Thompson didn't quite have that skill set. But we had seen this time and time again, a player with great scoring ability. That didn't mean you were going to win.

What Michael did was take it to another level—his persona, the way he looked and carried himself, how companies embraced him and put him in ads, that made him a star. He was intimidating for opponents, but he was likeable to everyone else. He was a crossover personality. The NBA wasn't crossing over much at the time; the NBA was really only for basketball fans. Magic and Bird started to change that, and Michael was the final step in terms of that, being popular all across the country and becoming not just a basketball star, but a global icon.

Michael started that wave, bringing in fans who would not normally watch the NBA, and they watched and loved him regardless of his pitfalls. And he had some early on in his career—he went seven years and couldn't win a title; he went seven years and alienated teammates because he refused to trust them. It wasn't until Phil Jackson came along and said, "You know what? We're going to take the ball out of your hands. We're going to trust it with Scottie Pippen, we are going to run a triangle offense, and you're going to get your touches. But other guys are going to get some touches, too." That is what did it; that took them to another level, where he started winning championships. Once he started going to the Finals that just raised his persona even more. He started really doing his thing, and he did it as well as anybody ever has—he won all six of them that he went to.

But I always think about that card game. He knew the whole time he wanted Tom Chambers and me and Ty to be out of the game, and he was going to go off. That's the difference with a guy like that, the way he always wanted that competitive edge. A guy like Michael is a rarity. Magic Johnson, Larry Bird, LeBron James, Kobe Bryant—there are only a handful of those guys and they are in a different stratosphere. Michael has his own stratosphere.

Reggie Theus

Guard

Career: 1979–1991
Head Coaching Career: 2008–2009
Career Highlights: .... two-time All-Star

Michael Jordan vs. Reggie Theus										
Regular Season	Games	Wins	Losses	Win %	Field Goal %	PPG	Points (High)	RPG	APG	SPG
Jordan	21	12	9	57.1	54.0	37.3	52 (12/20/89)	6.5	5.4	2.5
Theus	21	9	12	42.9	43.5	15.2	28 (three times)	2.1	6.0	1.0

Theus was the Bulls' No. 1 pick in 1978 and spent the first five years of his 13-year NBA career in Chicago. He would later play for the Kings, Hawks, Magic, and Nets.

WHAT I SAY was that I was fifteen minutes away from being part of a dynasty in Chicago. It's funny to put it that way, but wow, yeah, it is not the easiest thing to think about, because it is true. I had been in Chicago five years until 1984, and the previous year, I had even been an All-Star and averaged 24 points.[17] We were not a very good team, we did not have good pieces, but individually, I was young and I thought I was developing.[18] I was, if you go back and look at the numbers.

But for whatever reason, Kevin Loughery, the coach at the time, he just did

---

[17] Theus was an All-Star for the second time during in the 1982–83 season, averaging 23.8 points a game.
[18] The 1982–83 Bulls would go 28–54 for the season.

not like me. To this day, I don't understand why. It started in training camp, right from the beginning, he wouldn't play me, he wouldn't put me in, he wanted to get rid of me. He benched me for a long time; we had all kinds of problems.

At the time, the Bulls had been through a lot of coaches—I had seven coaches in my first five seasons in Chicago. To give you an example, I played for Jerry Sloan, who you could tell was going to be a good coach; he was a good young coach at the time. He is a Hall of Famer. He had played for the Bulls, he was coaching the Bulls, and you didn't need to be Einstein to see he knew how to coach the game. He had the demeanor and the toughness to be an NBA coach, even though he was young and just getting started. But they got rid of him, that's just how things were at the time in Chicago before Michael got there. You had a sense that the owners, the coaches, no one really knew what was going on.

It was a tough situation. Fans in Chicago now probably don't realize what it was like before then, because they have had such a good organization for so long. But then, the franchise was very unstable, it is not like it became in the '90s and how it is now. I had good years; I just had two or three bad months under Kevin Loughery. I dropped from 24 points one year down to eight or nine points the next year, and I went through long stretches where I wasn't playing.

So on the night of the trading deadline in 1984, they had to either trade me by midnight or keep me the rest of the year, and even though it was obvious Loughery did not like me, I did not know he was going to trade me. I don't even think the owners knew. It happened late at night, I had no idea—it was just about fifteen minutes before the deadline when I got the call. He had traded me to Kansas City [Kings], for a big man, Steve Johnson. Because Kevin Loughery had me on the bench, that really dropped my trade value.[19]

---

[19] The Bulls traded Theus to the Kansas City Kings for Steve Johnson, a second-round pick in the 1984 draft (Greg Wiltjer), and two second round picks in the '85

It was just a few months later that they would have the third pick in the draft and they wound up drafting Michael Jordan. They wound up getting rid of Kevin Loughery that next year, and that's it, they go onto a dynasty. For me, then, I was fifteen minutes from playing with Michael Jordan.

I have always been attached to Michael in that way—in a way, I was Michael before Michael was there. I was their top scorer. The fans in Chicago were upset about them trading me and were actually chanting my name after the trade. But then Michael became who he is, so that stopped really quickly. You know, they had Michael Jordan, so it was, "Reggie who?" It's pretty funny to think back on. I don't blame them.

I have so much respect for Michael and what he accomplished, because when he came into the league, he was good but he wasn't all that when he first came in. He didn't shoot the ball great, the team wasn't good—he didn't have much help around him. It wasn't a team that you worried too much about. But you could see his athleticism, and more important, you could see his competitiveness. That was the thing that set him apart. No one knew how dedicated he was and how hard he was going to work to become the player that he eventually became, the one we all know today. It also helped that they got some talent in there around him. That was always the problem in Chicago at the time; they were relatively talent poor before that.

When he first came into the league, we used to back off of him. "Go ahead, shoot it." That's what you'd tell him. It took him about three years before he really started to turn that around. He started to be able to make that jumper, and that was it. Once he had that, forget it. That's when he became the player we all know.

Guys like Michael and Magic Johnson, athletic guys who were good with the ball like that, the key was to pick them up early. Michael was

---

draft (Mike Brittain and Ken Johnson). Steve Johnson would go on to finish that season in Chicago before being traded with Mike Brittain (the second round pick) to the San Antonio Spurs for Gene Banks.

good going either direction, and the one thing with a player who is good at getting to the basket, you don't want them to get their momentum going. You watch LeBron James now, he is the same way—once a guy like that gets a full head of steam, you can't stop him. You have to get in front of him early.

The thing about a great player like Michael, you are not really going to stop them. You don't go into a game planning on totally shutting him down—let's not fool ourselves, no one has ever really stopped Michael Jordan. You just want to make it as tough as you can on him, collectively as a team, make it tough. He is a good passer, he will find the open guy, so he is going to make your whole defense react when he has the ball, and then react again with a pass.

For me, I would always rather give up the jump shot to Michael than to have him drive to the basket. I was fortunate to play in the heyday of basketball; I played against Magic Johnson and Larry Bird and Hall of Fame players like that. But the difference between Michael and those guys is that Michael would embarrass you. If you made a mistake, he would not just pull up and take a jumper. He would dunk on you, on your entire team, and his tongue would be out, and he had the look and you just knew there was a chance you wind up on a poster. Larry or Magic, they would wind up with a layup or something.

Michael would try to embarrass you with a dunk, and the crowd would go crazy and he would fire up the whole team. You had to be cautious of everything you did with Michael on the floor. I used to play against George Gervin, and George was another guy—he wasn't powerful like Mike was—but he was the same way, if you made one mistake with George, he was going to get by you and make you pay. But George wasn't powerful the way Mike was. If you had to give something to Michael, you gave him the jump shot.

He would trash talk. But the trash talk was enormous in those days; a lot of guys would do it. He was a trash talker, but it was subtle. He would say little things to you after he beat you and he would remind you about it. Or he would tell you what he is going to do and then go do it. It was subtle. He wasn't as bad as Larry Bird—he would be rambling the whole time, you couldn't get him to stop. Michael picked his spots. He was good at it.

But it is funny to think back on, because for a few years there, they were always looking for a point guard to play with Michael. I could play the point, I could play shooting guard, it didn't bother me either way. If you had us both in the backcourt, wow, we would have been a unique pair back there, at his size (6-6) and mine (6-7), you don't see a lot of backcourts that big. That would have been a tough matchup for a lot of teams, especially when you started getting coaches in there like Doug Collins and Phil Jackson, who knew what they were doing.

That trade deadline was big. I was just fifteen minutes away from having a chance to be part of the whole Bulls dynasty.

Dell Curry also remembers a famous dunk by Jordan.

I remember he had a dunk against us in Charlotte. He crossed over Rex Chapman, then he climbed onto the back of Kelly Tripucka and put his forearm on the back of Kelly, who just trying to get out of his way. That dunk brought everybody off of both benches. That is the one play I still remember, and I still see that highlight every once in a while. They didn't give him the foul; but everybody was so enamored with the dunk they forget about giving him the and-one.

My relationship with him was strictly competitive. I don't think Michael had any kind of relationship with anybody other than his teammates when he was between the lines. And you knew that going in. He had no friends on the floor. But afterward, everybody was good.

I remember once I anticipated a pass, cut the passing lane off, and stole the ball that was supposed to go to him. He didn't chase me down. I was looking behind me to see if he would try to chase me down. I asked him about it later, and he just shrugged. But I knew not to bring it up again. You don't mess with him that way.

Robert Parish

Center

Career: 1977–1997
Career Highlights: .... nine-time All-Star, four-time
NBA Finals Champion, Inducted into the
Naismith Memorial Hall of Fame (2003)
Jordan Highlights: .... 1997 NBA Finals Champion

Michael Jordan vs. Robert Parish										
Regular Season	Games	Wins	Losses	Win %	Field Goal %	PPG	Points (High)	RPG	APG	SPG
Jordan	42	22	20	52.3	52.1	33.4	52 (11/9/88)	6.2	5.6	2.7
Parish	42	20	22	47.7	55.4	13	27 (11/14/86)	9.1	1.2	0.6

Playoffs	Games	Wins	Losses	Win %	Field Goal %	PPG	Points (High)	RPG	APG	SPG
Jordan	10	3	7	30.0	47.5	36.7	63 (4/20/86)	6.6	5.8	2.1
Parish	10	7	3	70.0	53.8	11.5	23 (4/17/86)	6.7	1.1	0.4

Parish was a center, part of the legendary Celtics teams of the 1980s. He was on the floor on a warm afternoon when Jordan went for 63 points in a first-round playoff game against the Bulls, one Chicago lost in double overtime. After the game, Parish's teammate, Larry Bird, claimed that it was "God disguised as Michael Jordan" scoring all those points.

EVERYBODY REMEMBERS THE 63-point game, and it was a really great individual performance. Obviously, at the time, Michael Jordan was the best scorer in the league; he was just scratching the surface of how good he would be. But really, our strategy was to let him score if that was what they were going to do. We (the Celtics) were a great team at the time, with Larry Bird and Kevin McHale, our guards were great, we had been to the Finals, and we had won championships. We won it two years before, then we lost to the Lakers the next year, and in 1986, we wound up winning it again. We won 67 games that year, we were really tough to beat at home, and they were just an okay team at that time. Michael Jordan was young, and they did not have Scottie Pippen or any of those guys.

So, K. C. Jones, he was our coach, and the way he approached it was that we were going to score a lot of points, and if you look at it, we did.[20] Our feeling was that, if we score 120 points, there is no way Michael Jordan is going to score 121. That seemed to be K. C.'s way of looking at it. We had too many weapons, and that Bulls team did not have much else besides Jordan. K. C. kept us in one-on-one coverage on Jordan, it did not matter how much he was scoring.

The first game of that series (Eastern Conference First Round), he had scored a lot in that one, too, on our home floor.[21] And some of the guys were wondering and asking K. C. if maybe we should stop playing him one-on-one, maybe we should double-team. And K. C. just sort of shook it off and said he would think about it. But that first game, we won by a lot (123–104) so, you can't really fault K. C. We had good one-on-one defenders like Dennis Johnson and Danny [Ainge] and Jerry Sichting. So K. C. just left it up to those guys to do the best they could on him and we did not let their other guys beat us.

It was a great individual performance. But look at our team. We swept them in that series, and we went on to win the championship that year. I think we did pretty well in terms of that.

---

[20] Boston averaged 126.7 points in their opening series against Chicago.

[21] Jordan had 49 points on 18-for-36 shooting in that game.

Hubie Brown

Head Coaching Career: 1975–87, 2003–05
Career Highlights: .... two-time NBA Coach of the Year

Over the course of thirteen years spent as an NBA head coach—and even longer as a broadcaster—Hubie Brown saw Jordan through every phase of his career. But it is the early matchups against Jordan, when Brown was coaching in New York, that stand out the most. Jordan always seemed to excel against the Knicks, and that started early in his career.

LET ME TELL you, I was such a great defensive coach that my teams managed to hold Michael Jordan to 50 points in three different games. That's real genius, right?

One of the greatest shots ever made, I saw it, was Michael falling out of bounds with three seconds on the clock to win a game. It was his third year,[22] but he had been out in his second season with a foot injury. We were in the old Chicago Stadium, we were going back and forth, we would tie it, and Michael Jordan would come down and give the Bulls the lead. Over and over.[23] The last

---

[22] The game was in November of 1986.
[23] Jordan finished the game scoring 18 consecutive points, and scored 40 total.

possession, we tied it up with eight or nine seconds on the clock. Doug Collins was coaching, he didn't call a timeout, he just got it to Michael. He takes it up the whole length of the floor, and—he was right in front of our bench—he raises up. He not only made the shot over Kenny Walker, who was two or three inches taller than Michael, but—you saw it time and again on the replay—Patrick Ewing comes into the picture, Gerald Wilkins comes into the picture. Michael is fading out of bounds and we have three guys on him, and he let it go as he was falling. Boom. They win the game. We had him double-teamed, we had him triple-teamed, but it didn't matter. He just kept scoring.

That is what always got me when people talk about a guy like Michael Jordan, especially before he won a championship and everyone was focused on what he couldn't do. I heard it over and over, "He hasn't got a jump shot." Oh yeah? He had a pretty good jump shot right from the beginning; you go back and look and see him hanging in the air and making those shots over people, he had a pretty good jump shot. He shot 52 percent from the field in his first year, and those were not all layups—he was shooting. Maybe the jumper was not as good as the shots he got driving to the hoop, but he had a jump shot.

But people kept telling him he could not shoot the jumper. So what did he do? He went out and became a world-class jump-shooter, just an unstoppable shooter from eight feet on out to 15, 16 feet. And he gave you not only the midrange jumper, but the fadeaway shot in the post. He made them at very high percentages, and never mind all the things he could do out of the post, where he could beat you and get to the rim, he could make that fadeaway and that was it. He was one of the [best] post-up players—at any position—in the league during his era. Okay, so you point out two things he can't do, give him a little time, and he comes back and is one of the best in the league at those two things. As a coach, you would want to double-team him, but at the same time, he became really good at reading the double team and using the players around him to expose it. You were running out of options if you're trying to guard him.

You respected Michael because, not only did he love the competition, but because of the excellence. Because when he retired, you have to remember now, not only the points per game—30 points—but the six rebounds, the five assists, the 50 percent shooting. That is excellence right there, all-around excellence. He was always able to go off the dribble; he could beat his man going in either direction. And then he made himself a great shooter and a great post-up player. And then, when he decided to make himself into a great defensive player, you were talking about a guy . . . for years people said he was only a scorer, but there he was, All-Defense every single year.[24]

That's what I loved about watching him as he got more and more mature. When you look at the greatest players of all time, when I was a coach and over the years, doing television, I really respect the guys who can defend, who make themselves into elite-level defensive players. There are only two players I have seen who you could classify as "double-teamers" on defense: Michael Jordan and John Stockton. By that I mean, no matter where the play was, if there was a guy who went into the post or even on the other side of the floor, Jordan would leave his man—even if it was a scorer—he would leave and double-team the post, because he had such incredibly quick hands and quick reactions, he knew he could create turnovers and get into the fast break going the other way.

It was a big part of his game; he was always in the top five in steals. The only other player like that was John Stockton, who would do the same thing. That is the ultimate affirmation of your ability as a defensive player. Jordan's coaches had so much faith in him that they would let him double-team at that angle and still get back to the guy he was guarding—and Jordan was guarding one of the top scorers in the league just about every single night. Never mind what he was doing for the team offensively, he was still doing it defensively as well. If you're

---

[24] Jordan would be named to the NBA All-Defensive team nine times during his career, as well as being named the 1988 NBA Defensive Player of the Year.

a player on that team and you are going to be lazy on defense and you look up and see what Michael is doing? You are not going to be lazy anymore, Jack.

If Michael Jordan were playing today, he would absolutely dominate. People today don't understand that. Today, you no longer have hand-checking, and when Michael was playing, defenders were allowed to reach out and put their hand on your hip. They could move you, and if you tried to get by them, they could stick out the forearm and say, "No, you can't go that way." Now, because the league wants scoring, you can't use the hand-check. Now the guards have a green light to get to the basket. It's an easy path to the basket, and a defender has got to play them perfectly without the hand contact or the forearm. Or else you are not keeping him in front of you. If you don't know what it was like to play in the 1980s, going against those defensive players, go back and watch some of those old games. If you wanted to get to the rim, you were going to take contact; you were going to get hit. Watch Michael Jordan against the Bad Boys in Detroit. He got hit, he got hit hard, he got hit a lot. You don't have that in today's game.

Everybody has got a different opinion of who is the best and all of that. It depends on who you talk to, right? I think Michael Jordan is the greatest ever to play the game, but someone else, someone who is only watching basketball now, might say, "No, LeBron James is better." Okay, but there is an older guy who is probably going to tell you that Oscar Robertson was better than both of them. But for me, it's Jordan. What he accomplished in his time, I don't think is something you can match or that will be matched for a long time.

Section Two: Breaking Through

"Chuck [Daly] spoke up and said, 'This stuff ain't going to work. It ain't going to work.' . . . Basically, the idea was, double-team him every time he got it, or triple-team or send four if we need to, and pray that the other guys were not going to be good enough."

—Pistons assistant coach Brendan Suhr

BEGINNING IN 1986–87, Michael Jordan began a run in which he would lead the league in scoring for four straight years, take home an MVP award, and earn All-Star and first-team All-NBA selections in each season. But through the end of the 1980s, while the individual accolades piled up, Jordan still dealt with consistent criticism—that he was a big-time scorer but could never win a championship. As one headline in a Chicago paper read in 1988: "Jordan Wins MVP Award, But It Doesn't Have a Ring To It."

There was little doubt as to why Jordan remained without a championship trophy in those seasons—or even without a spot in the NBA Finals. That was the Detroit Pistons, the team that eliminated the Bulls in 1988, '89, and '90, the final two defeats coming in the Eastern Conference Finals. Detroit had earned its reputation as the "Bad Boys," with their physical play, and they were especially tough on Jordan, believing that if the defense pushed Jordan around and hounded him enough with double-teams, he would wear down and be physically unable to carry the team in late-game situations.

While some players would have accepted their lot, Jordan took the physical punishment from the Pistons as a call to bulk up his own body, and he began doing that in earnest in the early 1990s, working with trainer Tim Grover. The work paid off—not only did Jordan and the

Bulls finally beat the Pistons, but he led the team to three consecutive championships, something that had not been done since the Celtics dynasty of the mid-1960s.

This section highlights those battles Jordan had with the Pistons, the work he did on and off the court to change his own fortunes, and the championships he won against the Lakers, Blazers, and Suns after that.

Tim Grover

As a renowned trainer in Chicago, Tim Grover wrote the book on how Michael Jordan got into the kind of shape he needed to be in to handle the physical play of the Detroit Pistons. Literally—Grover's book, Jump Attack, *details the regimen he used with Jordan in the early '90s, and how he kept Jordan in top condition thereafter.*

I FIRST MET MICHAEL in 1989. I was young, twenty-four or twenty-five years old. I grew up in Chicago and had the opportunity to play at a mid-major school there. I got my degree in kinesiology and my master's, and I was working at a gym after I had gotten done in school. I

was there at the gym, and I had read a small newspaper article about how Michael Jordan was tired of getting beaten up by the Detroit Pistons every year in the playoffs and he was trying to figure out what he could do. I thought I could help.

I had been trying to get on with the Bulls for pretty much the whole time after I finished college. I wrote letters, made phone calls, I did it all. People told me I was crazy, that it would be impossible. But when I saw that article, I got in touch with the team physician, that was Dr. John Hefferon at that time, and the athletic trainer, Mark Pfeil. I told them, this is what I do, this is what I can accomplish, and this is my background. Michael told them, "Okay, I want to meet this kid." They brought me in to the practice facility and I had a thirty-minute meeting with Michael there.

When I met him, I knew I was going to have to be very thorough, very fast, and very professional. I knew this was a big chance. I laid out what I wanted to do for him. He was skeptical, he thought it was too good to be true, that the program I had in mind was not going to work. But he agreed to give it a try. He told me I had thirty days. But thirty days turned into fifteen years.

Michael was different, what we were doing was different. He was the first person in a professional sport to hire a trainer like me, as an individual, and have me available to him 24/7. That's what I wrote about in *Relentless*—a lot of people think that the best in their fields, in basketball or business or whatever, are the ones who are so good that they don't need help. But the opposite is true. Someone like Michael was constantly looking for help, for ways to get better and find out new information.

What was unique about the situation is, we would do a workout and I would tell Michael how he was going to feel twenty-four hours after the workout, forty-eight hours after the workout, seventy-two hours after. I would tell him, "This is what we are going to do today and this is how you are going to feel today and the day after that." Once he understood that I knew exactly what was going on with his body and how to get those end results, trust came along very quickly. That was good for me. I did not have a whole lot of time to show him what I was capable of doing, so I wanted him to understand what we were doing with each step, what was going on. I wanted him to know I knew what he was feeling physically. I mean, I had thirty days.

Ultimately, it was all about the Detroit Pistons. They were tough. Joe Dumars was a strong defender, and they had guys who would knock you over if you went to the rim. They were beating him up. That was the reason he wanted to do all of this, that was the goal . . . that was his end result. He had done enough on an individual level, but he knew that in order to get to that championship level, he had to go through Detroit and figure out a way to be able to play consistently in the playoffs against a team that was just really physical; a team that took being physical to a whole new level. He knew that, instead of just taking it, he had to be able to dish it out. Instead of them hitting him first, he would hit them.

The key to what we were doing was to keep Michael fresh throughout the season. That was going to help him be tougher when the playoffs came. This is a problem that is prevalent even these days—you have athletes in all sports—not just basketball—they spend a lot of time training in the off-season. They will get themselves in great shape, they will work on a certain skill to try to improve their game, they will add muscle or lose weight or whatever it is. And that's valuable. But seasons, in every sport, are extremely long, with the preseason, with the playoffs, all of it. They require a lot of time. What happens is, in every physical game that you play, if you don't continue to work on it, on a consistent basis, you are going to lose all of that progress every year. So you see players who start a season looking one way and actually finish it looking completely, completely different. That is what was happening with Michael, and we had to change it.

That's how the "Breakfast Club" got started. It was something we wanted to make part of the routine. I had a chef who would come to Michael's house and make breakfast, and it was like, breakfast was the reward for the workout. After every single game or every single practice or team meeting, I would find Michael and ask, "5, 6, or 7?" Meaning, are we working out at 5 in the morning or 6 or 7? He would shoot back the time, and I would show up at the house. He would be ready to go, Scottie Pippen would be ready to go, and Ron Harper would be ready to go. Sometimes there were others, but those three were there all the time. They were the Breakfast Club. They motivated each other. There are days when you might be tired or a little sick, but they pushed each other at those times. Michael viewed practice as something that should be harder than the game, and he approached it that way.

We would go through this extensive workout, anywhere from an hour to two hours, depending on whether there was a game. We would go through the whole workout in the gym at Michael's house, and then we would go upstairs and have breakfast. And we'd just sit and talk about the game they had coming up, who they were playing, the strategy, and they'd get their mental focus locked in. But in order to get breakfast, you had to work out. If one of the guys decided to skip the workout and just show up at the house to eat, no breakfast for them. He could sit there and watch everyone else eat. They would finish breakfast, then leave his house and go right to practice.

Getting into that routine was very important for them. That's where you see the level, the mentality of a player like that—he wants to be focused on getting better every day, have it be part of the everyday routine. When I was writing my book *Relentless*, which is where a lot of that came from—being around a guy like Michael for so long and seeing how he was; watching him prepare for a game not only physically, but mentally. Prepare for practice, what he would do after the game, all of that. I got a chance to sit down with and talk and see not only the greatest basketball player, but the greatest competitor ever, and watch his preparation for everything he did. And I got to be able to sit down and discuss it with him and say, "Why did you make this play? Why did you pass that ball?" When you talk about the mind of a champion, he's the first person that comes to mind: Michael Jordan. It is a mental thing that you can use for anything in life.

You have to pay attention to the small stuff, the details do matter. For example, Michael was impeccable with the way he dressed, and that was not an accident. That was something that he felt he wanted to project to his teammates in the locker room and also to the guys he was playing against. He wanted his opponents to look at him like he was someone who didn't have any flaws, so the clothes he would wear, the cars that he drove, everything was systematically laid out and there was a reason behind everything he did. He was trying to get the upper hand, all the time.

I called him a black cat because of the effect he had when he crossed your path. It was not going to be a good thing for you. He would go into the opponents' locker room before games to talk to someone, and he would just change the dynamic in there. It is a fear and respect thing. He never cared about being liked; he did not need to be friends with everyone all over the league. He did want to be feared and respected, though. That was important.

So, you can imagine, he walks into your locker room and everyone else now stops and looks. They're not thinking about their game plan anymore and what they're supposed to be doing, and their focus is just gone. Michael Jordan is here. So the focus is on him and what he's wearing and who he's talking to and what he's doing. And right before he would leave, he always knew who was going to guard him in that game. So he would make sure he gave a nice little stare at him before he walked out. That's where he would get that mental edge.

It would drive other coaches crazy, the opposing coaches were not happy about that, of course. But you know what? There was not a security person in the world that was going to stop Michael Jordan from entering whatever locker room he wanted to go into.

Unfortunately, you can't do that anymore—they don't allow opponents in the locker rooms the way they used to. When you have an individual like Michael, as influential as he was, when they said he changed all the rules, sometimes they mean it literally. They changed that locker room rule because of him. The NBA had to change a lot of rules because of the little things he would do in order to get an advantage over people.

Ultimately, he was able to do it. He saw that wall, the Detroit Pistons, and he got through it. I think he had a lot of respect for them in the end, even though they were so physical with him and didn't always show the best as far as sportsmanship goes. When we first started, his goal was to get past the Detroit Pistons and he did it. He knew that he needed them to push him to that next level. And then from there, everything took off. I wouldn't say it got easier for him, because he actually worked harder and harder as he went on. But he had a better understanding, he trusted me more, he trusted his body more. He understood what was working.

He won three championships in a row, then retired, came back, and won three more. Not many players could have done that. I have always said that, if he had not retired in the first place, he would have eight championships. I really believe that. There are a whole lot of players, like Reggie Miller or Patrick Ewing or Charles Barkley, who could have won championships, but were not able to because they were sort of blocked from getting those rings by Michael. They were just in the wrong generation.

I don't think there was really any comparison for him, even now. I think what he was doing then was ahead of his time; he really changed the way a whole lot of players after him approach the game, approach any game. He brought a different level of commitment to everything he did. He was that focused on winning.

But when it was over, when he retired, after fifteen years of these difficult, hard workouts at all these early hours—and I wrote this in the book—he told me, "If I ever see you in my neighborhood again, I am going to shoot you." That made me laugh, and I can understand that, enough is enough. Time to go.

Phil Hubbard

Forward

Career: **1980–1989**

Michael Jordan vs. Phil Hubbard									
Regular Season	**Games**	**Wins**	**Losses**	**Win %**	**Field Goal %**	**PPG**	**Points (High)**	**RPG**	**APG**	**SPG**
Jordan	19	9	10	47.4	51.5	32.9	52 (12/17/87)	5.0	5.5	2.7
Hubbard	19	10	9	52.6	53.0	12.6	25 (2/21/88)	5.3	0.9	0.8
Playoffs	**Games**	**Wins**	**Losses**	**Win %**	**Field Goal %**	**PPG**	**Points (High)**	**RPG**	**APG**	**SPG**
Jordan	4	2	2	50.0	51.2	43.3	55 (5/1/88)	5.8	6.0	1.0
Hubbard	4	2	2	50.0	16.7	0.5	2 (4/28/88)	0.8	0.0	0.0

Hubbard played 10 seasons in the NBA, spending the bulk of his career with Cleveland and finishing with averages of 10.9 points and 5.3 rebounds. He participated as an NBA player in the scrimmages leading up to the 1984 Olympic games.

I REMEMBER PLAYING MICHAEL Jordan when he first came into the league, because I was with Cleveland and so we saw Chicago a lot, as our teams were in the same division. We had World B. Free at that time, and he was one of the really good scorers in the league, a real high-output scorer. He was getting older, though, in his thirties. Michael was a rookie at that time, and was still feeling his way around. He had to guard World and he struggled to stop him—but he was able to score with him, and that was something else.

First game we saw him, World got 30 points that night against Michael, but

Jordan had a big game, too.[1] Though defensively, you could see World knew how to beat him. The first time we played up against him, you could see that the scoring was there, the effort and energy was there, but he was not the defensive player that he would eventually become. You couldn't tell he would lift up his entire game.

Of course, he did. And if you go from where he was back when I first played against him in the NBA, in 1984, to where I wound up my career in 1989, in Cleveland, you could see that he had really just gotten so good in all aspects of his game. That was the year that he made "The Shot," the one that really put him up in front of everybody, the one everybody in Cleveland still remembers. If you go back and look at that year, we were a good team, we had beaten them six times that year, and some of those wins were by 15, 16 points or more. Six times in the regular season, we handled them. We had won 57 games, so, we were a pretty good team.[2]

We went into that first-round series against the Bulls, it was when you had five-game series in the first round. I did not like that. It put the favorite at a disadvantage and made luck more of a factor. For us, the big problem was that Mark Price had gotten a concussion maybe ten days before when we had been playing the Pistons. He got hit in the head with an elbow from Rick Mahorn and received a concussion. So, the first game, Mark Price did not play, and I thought, for us, that changed the whole series. Mark was a damn good point guard and that changed the series.

We came out and we were not in our normal rhythm and lost the game after beating them six straight during the regular season. That gives you a little bit of a mental edge in a playoff series, but you lose the first game, and that edge is gone. They won one game at our place, and we

---

[1] Jordan scored 45 points in his debut against Cleveland, his highest-scoring game to that point, on 20-for-33 shooting, with 11 assists. The Bulls would win the game, 112–108.

[2] The Cavaliers won those six games by an average of 12 points, with their largest margin of victory at 24 (a 115–91 win on March 15, 1989).

went and won one at their place, so we were 2–2. And they came in for that final Game 5 and even then, we thought we had them. They had to come to our place and play, and they were a young team. They would not be able to handle the playoff pressure, we figured.

We were winning Game 5 with three seconds to go, and all we had to do was not let them get a clean look. Michael got the ball up on the right wing and got into the middle, and he made that shot at the last second, he wound up pulling that one out for them. That was my last game, I retired after that season. I suppose I went out with a memorable game, but you know—a memorable game for who? A memorable game for Chicago. I would rather forget it, but it is one of those highlights that you always see at least once a year, even more than once a year for a few years there. Watching Michael making that shot against Craig Ehlo in Game 5, there is just nothing you can do. I kind of feel bad for Craig, because he was a good defensive player, a very good defender. But most people only know him because of that shot.

What a lot of people don't know about that shot is what happened in Game 4; that game went into overtime in Chicago. He was unbeliev-able in that game. He scored 50 points, but he missed some free throws late in the game and the rest of the team didn't give him a lot of help. At the end of regulation, he had a chance to win it; it would have been over right there in Game 4 in the old Chicago Stadium. He went up and in the last seconds of regulation, took a baseline shot, a jumper to win that game. And he missed it. So the game went into overtime and we won.

But think about it—ever since then, all his game-winning shots have been in the middle of the floor, around the free-throw area. If you go back and check, you will see. The next game, the shot against us in Cleveland, was right at the free-throw line. The Bryon Russell shot against Utah, he was at the free-throw line. Look at the game-winners he hits, he is always on the wing or at the free-throw line. He does not shoot from the baseline in those situations. The big ones, when he needed a basket, it was in the middle of the floor, kind of driving toward that free-throw line and pulling up for a jumper, or he would make a play for somebody else by penetrating to that spot. I think that started with us, he developed a comfort zone in that free-throw line area. But the baseline, I really think he tried that against us that time and did not want to try it again, not for a jumper.

We underestimated them, I would say that. We were expected to win that series, and I think what you saw for the first time that year was the way Michael responded to expectations, the way he used that to play a little better. Even their own writers were picking us to win that series. That motivated him extremely, to show that he was at least going to go out with a fight. But expectations and what actually happens, they're not always the same thing.

He was not a great player then. No one would have considered him that; he was not on the level of Magic Johnson or Larry Bird. But he was on the way to being a great player, I think that game or that series was one that helped him get there. That was one of the years they lost to the Pistons in the Eastern Conference Finals. He just continued to get better each year, each playoff series he played in the years after that. They started getting further and further in the playoffs and everyone started seeing him as more than just a guy who could score.

By the end, that had changed, of course. He just became a monster at both ends of the floor. He was always so efficient with his shots, his layups, and his free throws. He knew how to get his points efficiently, scoring a number of different ways. He became a great defensive player, won those championships. To me, he became the best player in the history of the league.

While it was a tough blow for Ehlo, he is happy to say that it no longer burdens him.

I was bummed about it at the time. But now it is fun for me to watch. Kids come up to me all the time, asking, "Are you the guy who was guarding Michael Jordan?" Outside of losing the game, there really have been no negatives about Michael's shot for me. I love talking about it.

Larry Nance was in front of him, and I was standing close, between him and the basket. We were double-teaming him on the inbounds play. Michael stepped in toward me and then out and got the pass from Brad Sellers. He went right and took Larry with him, then went left and I was the only one in front of him. He stopped just in time, I guess, and put the shot up. I was still running and went by him with my hand aimed at his face. I looked back and saw it on the way, and knew it looked good. I thought it hit the rim, which it did, but it went in anyway. And I went down and pounded the floor.

James Edwards

Center

Career: 1978–1996
Career Highlights: .... three-time NBA Finals Champion
Jordan Highlights: .... 1996 NBA Finals Champion

Michael Jordan vs. James Edwards										
Regular Season	Games	Wins	Losses	Win %	Field Goal %	PPG	Points (High)	RPG	APG	SPG
Jordan	22	8	14	36.4	49.9	31.8	54 (11/20/92)	7.0	6.5	2.0
Edwards	22	14	8	63.6	47.9	9.3	21 (3/16/90)	3.2	0.4	0.1

Playoffs	Games	Wins	Losses	Win %	Field Goal %	PPG	Points (High)	RPG	APG	SPG
Jordan	22	10	12	45.5	48.1	30	36 (5/12/88)	6.7	6.1	2.1
Edwards	22	12	10	54.5	45.3	7.3	16 (twice)	2.8	0.5	0.0

James "Buddha" Edwards played for eight different NBA teams over 19 seasons, a teammate to players from Kareem Abdul-Jabbar to Isiah Thomas to, finally, Jordan himself. It was in Detroit with the "Bad Boys" that Edwards had his most memorable moments, though, as part of the wave of bench players that separated the Pistons from so many other teams.

I THINK A LOT of it started with Chuck Daly. He was an excellent coach, and he understood how to really motivate his players. The way we saw it was, the Bulls were a one-man team, they were Michael Jordan and that was all. They did not have a whole lot else they were working with. So Chuck and Ronny Rothstein, who kind of helped Chuck come up with those defenses, they really had us focused on Michael and stopping him.

Those series were very memorable. We did not like the Bulls. The Bulls did not like us. Everybody knew that, and I don't think anyone tried to hide it or anything. We won the Eastern Conference championship three straight times, and we knew they were trying to get our spot. We had to go up against them three years in a row, and we were able to beat them every time. It was only in the fourth year that they finally figured out how to beat us. And I will say this for them: when they did figure it out, they really figured it out. In that last series we had with them, in 1991, they beat us four straight. They took it to us that year.

We were a very physical team, it was not just with Michael Jordan, but with everyone we played. You had Rick Mahorn, of course, and you had Bill Laimbeer out there, Dennis Rodman played physical, I played physical. That's just the way we played—a lot of teams played physical back then, like Boston, the New York Knicks, even the Lakers. Maybe we got the most notoriety for it; maybe we did it a little more than most teams did. And, the series we had against Michael Jordan and the Bulls, it got a lot of attention. But the league as a whole was more physical back then. It's not like it is now where you get a flagrant foul every time you touch somebody.

I played against a lot of great players, but Michael Jordan in those years, he was most definitely the best player I played against. Whenever we faced him, that was when the "Jordan Rules" came about—we wanted to stop him and let the other guys score. We were not going to let Michael Jordan beat us, whatever it takes. Let somebody else beat us. Double-team. Triple-team. As long as it was not Michael. We were able to do that, until 1991, they just were really good that year. A lot was made about, after we lost, whether we shook hands with them or not. We had just passed the torch to them. I don't think they cared whether we shook their hands. That was more the media making a big deal of it.

I closed out my career in Chicago with Michael and the Bulls in 1996, and I was able to be part of a team that made history. We won a championship, we won 72 games. I was playing behind Luc Longley and Bill Wennington, but I was happy to be playing a role. You can score 30 points a game, but if you're not winning, it is sort of hollow. A lot of young guys come into the league, and it takes them a while to realize that. Some guys never realize it. I had been around for nineteen years, and you wind up playing with all kinds of teammates if you're around that long.

So I was not too worried about going to Chicago and being one of those old Pistons—Michael, Scottie Pippen, Phil Jackson, they just wanted players who could help them win. I never really had anything against the Bulls or Michael or anything. They didn't have anything against me as long as I was helping them win. It was the same with Dennis Rodman. They brought him in that year, too, and that turned out to be a great move for everyone. Dennis is in the Hall of Fame now.[3]

I enjoyed playing with him. I was a big guy who used the fadeaway jump shot a lot as a big part of my game. It made it difficult for other big men to block, which is why I liked the fadeaway. Michael would always say he could block it, because he would try to sneak in and get the ball from behind. As he got older, if you remember, he used that fadeaway a lot. It got some good use from him.

The thing that stands out is that Michael was as mentally tough as anyone. I think that goes back to playing against us in those Pistons days. We toughened him up, we put him through some things physically that made him get better. He got stronger and stronger every year. The bumping, at first, it fazed him. It made it difficult on him. But he got to a point where he didn't even care. He would shrug it off and keep playing. And then, even more than that, he got to a point where he was the one doing the bumping. That's when he was really at his best. That's when he really became the greatest player in the league.

---

[3] Rodman was inducted into the Naismith Memorial Basketball Hall of Fame in 2011.

Brendan Suhr

A long and varied career in coaching landed Suhr in Detroit in the late '80s, where he was an assistant to Chuck Daly and witnessed the Pistons' legendary battles against Jordan and the Bulls.

IJOINED THE PISTONS a shade into January 1989. They had already gotten their reputation as the "Bad Boys" and had been in the Finals against the Lakers the previous year. It was really the height of the NBA, because you still had the Celtics and Lakers, you had the Bulls on the rise, and you had great teams all over the East. And you had us, the Bad Boys. We embraced the reputation. As the story goes, it was actually a promo tape that the league had done on the four best teams from the year before, and that is where the Bad Boys thing started. The league had this tape and on the label it said, "Bad Boys." And it was the Pistons tape. So they ran with it.

I had been with Atlanta, on the bench with Mike Fratello, but Stan Kasten, the owner at the time, moved me off the bench and was grooming me to be general manager eventually. Ronny Rothstein had gone to Miami to be the first head coach of the Heat in the off-season, and then Dick Versace had become the head coach with the Pacers in early January. So Chuck Daly had an opening and asked me to come and take it. We had a very good team in Atlanta at the time, but it was a great opportunity to join the staff in Detroit.

I remember I said to Chuck, "You guys lost the Finals last year by two points. I am afraid I might screw it up." And Chuck gave me the best answer he possible could, saying "Listen, I have been coaching for thirty-four years. I have made every mistake you can make in coaching. Just come and let's have some fun."

And I'm glad I did. We were not the best team in the East at that point. The Cavs were, Lenny Wilkens's Cavs—Mark Price, Ron Harper, Craig Ehlo, Brad Daugherty, "Hot Rod" Williams. They were killing everyone. They were running away with it. They were a great team. And the next thing you know, we make the big trade, Adrian Dantley for Mark Aguirre. The next time we played the Cavs after that, Mark Price, you know, "ran into" Rick Mahorn's forearm and got a concussion. He was not right the rest of the year. We went 41–8 down the stretch; it was an unbelievable team. We were like sharks once we got within the Cavs; we smelled blood in the water. And we just ran by them. We won 63 games.

Everyone remembers that year as Pistons vs. Bulls in the Eastern Conference Finals, but honestly, it was not supposed to be that way. It was the Cavs, at that time, more than the Pistons and Bulls. But once Price was hurt they had a hard time. And that was when they lost to Michael Jordan on that famous shot in the first round, the one where Craig Ehlo was guarding him.

The real irony of that was that the team we could not beat that year—sometimes you run into that, a team that the matchups are wrong and you just can't beat them—was New York, with Rick Pitino. We had trouble with their press. No other teams ran a press like that. We turned the ball over against them, 18, 19 times per game. They beat us four out of four during the season, and by a pretty good margin. We could not beat New York. We were going to play them in the conference finals, they were the second seed. I am not sure we would have beaten them.[4]

We were not thinking about the Bulls. We were worried about the Knicks. But damn, wouldn't you know, Chicago upsets them in the second round. The Bulls were a good team at the time, but they were the No. 6 seed and did us the favor of taking out the Cavs and the Knicks. Those were the No. 2 and No. 3 teams in the standings.

So we faced Chicago in that Eastern Conference Finals and won that, no doubt, because of the "Jordan Rules." Even prior to that, the Pistons had dominated Michael. It was the year before that they started just being really, really physical with him and did a good job with him. The whole idea was to double-team or triple-team him and force him to pass the ball. He might score 35 or 40, but it would take its toll on him, and a lot of games we'd still win by 15.

But that was starting to change in 1989. They had Horace Grant, they had Scottie Pippen—he was in his second year, had become a starter, and was becoming a very good player. They were getting better and better. We went into the Conference Finals and we were the hot team, we had swept the first round against Boston and swept the second round against Milwaukee. So we had not lost a playoff game going into the Conference Finals. We had almost a full week off and at the same time, the Bulls were battling it out with the Knicks in seven games. They won their series on a Friday night. That meant our series was going to open on Sunday afternoon in Detroit, which gave us a huge advantage.

We had plenty of rest, but they came in and stole Game 1 from us. In the first quarter, they just came in and put us on our heels. We had been off so long, we just could not catch up to them. Michael was phenomenal; he had 32 points in that opener.

---

[4] During the 1988–89 season, the Knicks were 4–0 against the Pistons, with average scores of 106.3–97.3. The Pistons averaged 17.75 turnovers a game, with a high of 24 (12/22/88) and a low of 11 (1/11/89).

We won Game 2, but in Game 3 we were up 19 points on their home floor [in the first half]. Okay, so we were going to get control of the series back, we were winning the whole way . . . but then Jordan goes for 46 points. He leads them on this comeback, he is getting into the lane, he is getting space to shoot the ball. Laimbeer gets called for an offensive foul, and Jordan makes a shot off the glass at the last second. They win by two points. That was when the Jordan Rules really happened, in the middle of that night. The next day, we are all talking about it and coming up with ideas on how to deal with Michael Jordan. Isiah, myself, Joe Dumars, everyone was getting involved.

But Chuck spoke up and said, "This stuff ain't going to work. It ain't going to work." We had the two best defensive players in the league in Dennis Rodman and Joe Dumars, and we still couldn't stop Michael. So basically, the idea was to double-team him every time he got [the ball], or triple-team or send four if we needed to, and pray that the other guys—John Paxson and Craig Hodges and those guys—were not going to be good enough.

You had to send him into the middle, where Laimbeer and Mahorn were. If you were guarding Michael and he got by you, you had to make sure he felt it, give him some contact. And once he got into the lane, he got more contact from our big guys. We felt we had enough depth that we could wear him down. And we did that. We wore him down. And the other players on the Bulls gagged like crazy. We were lucky, we either fouled Mike or he passed the ball. He took a lot of free throws that next game and in that series, that was part of the game plan.[5] Their guys could not make a shot. So we went from being down 2–1 to turning it around and winning three straight. We swept the Lakers that year, too, so those two games we lost to the Bulls were the only ones we lost that entire postseason.

That was when you were allowed to play that way; you could be physical, you could have a no-layup rule. That was the way you played

---

[5] Jordan took 79 foul shots in six games, hitting 60 of them for a 75.9 FT%.

playoff basketball. Now there would be flagrant fouls all over the pl.
it's a joke. A lot of people maybe think of those Pistons teams as dirt,
but we were within the rules at the time. And Michael Jordan has said
that, it was because of us that he hired Tim Grover and changed his
body and got stronger. In the long run, he was a better player for it, and
those Bulls-Pistons series were some terrific matchups.

**Isiah Thomas, who would become close with Jordan, had a few thoughts
on him during their time as opponents.**

We were fierce, fierce competitors, and I think he and I both loved
competing like that. But we've always respected each other. I've never
heard Michael Jordan say one bad thing about me. You've never heard
me say one bad thing about Michael Jordan. Everyone else has said we
don't like one another, but I've never read or said a thing.

He was such a complete player on both ends. He was a great foul
shooter, he turned into a 3-point shooter. He had midrange game. He
had a low post game. He was a lock down defender. He was one of
the best.

Larry Drew

Guard

NBA Career: 1981–91
Head Coaching Career: 2011–14

Michael Jordan vs. Larry Drew										
Regular Season	Games	Wins	Losses	Win %	Field Goal %	PPG	Points (High)	RPG	APG	SPG
Jordan	6	5	1	83.3	52.6	30.5	37 (12/19/89)	6.7	6.3	1.2
Drew	6	1	5	16.7	40.0	8.0	17 (1/29/85)	0.5	2.5	0.3
Playoffs	Games	Wins	Losses	Win %	Field Goal %	PPG	Points (High)	RPG	APG	SPG
Jordan	4	3	1	75.0	56.7	31.5	36 (6/2/91)	7.3	11.8	2.3
Drew	4	1	3	25.0	37.5	1.8	4 (6/5/91)	0.5	0.0	0.0

Before making his mark as a coach, Drew played 11 seasons professionally in the NBA and overseas, finishing his career as a backup point guard behind Magic Johnson with the Lakers. That lent him a front-row seat to the 1991 Finals.

GOING INTO THAT series (the 1991 NBA Finals), I just remember, it was two really good teams. It was sort of the end of the run for the Lakers; Kareem [Abdul-Jabbar] was retired, Pat Riley was gone, Mike Dunleavy was the coach. We were still a good team. Michael Jordan had not won a championship at that point; he had been focused on getting past the Pistons all those years. They finally did it that year, they swept the Pistons. They came into the

Finals and they had lost only one game in the playoffs coming in.[6] Th
were playing really, really well. But they had never won a championship

We started on the road for Game 1 in Chicago and came up with a big win; it was a close game.[7] That was at Chicago Stadium, which was a tough place to play on the road. Michael had a chance to tie that game late, but he missed a jumper and we were able to win. But after that game, it just seemed like Michael took the series over. They beat us in Game 2 in Chicago and went back and beat us three straight games in LA. He just played at a really, really high level. Their whole team just seemed to play really well—they had Scottie Pippen, they had Horace Grant, who was a really good player for them. But it was Michael who set the tone, I thought, not just on the offensive end but on the defensive end as well. They were one of the best defensive teams in the league at the time.

Michael was quiet for the first half of Game 2,[8] but then I remember him just getting hot. It was like, you knew he was going to get it going. He couldn't miss, he made all these shots in a row.[9] Also, remember, it was Game 2 where he made that drive that ended up as a commercial, the one everyone talks about—he hung up in the air and switched hands in midair, laying it up on the other side of the rim.

I was actually sitting near the end of the court when he came down the middle and made that circus shot. I had the best look at it, and it was incredible. The way he came down the middle and after he switched hands in the air and laid it up off the other side, first of all it was a phenomenal shot. Only a guy with that kind of hang time could have performed that shot. He shot it as if he was expecting someone to come and challenge it, but he was up so high, it was like he did not realize that there was no one else in the league that was going to be able

---

[6] They had lost Game 3 of the Eastern Conference Semifinals to the Philadelphia 76ers.
[7] The Lakers won 93–91.
[8] Jordan scored only two points in the first twenty minutes of the game.
[9] He hit 13 consecutive shots.

get up that high. To this day, people are still talking about that shot; it was really remarkable.

The crowd blew up when they saw that. The place was just full of excitement. Their team blew up. For us, we were kind of stunned. They were already up by a big margin. All you could do was shake your head. But a guy to be able to make that kind of a move and then finish the basket; the crowd was already into the game, but Michael basically took the game over. That was just the part everyone remembers, but it was more than just that shot. He took the game over on both ends of the floor. He was playing with a lot of aggression, against us, against Magic Johnson. They made it hard on Magic—they had Michael on him at times, then they would take him off and have Scottie on him. Their whole game plan was to wear Magic down, and they did it. It was not just the offensive end where Michael was so good; he was doing it on defense, too.

It was something to see him at that stage of his career, when he was young and really at his peak. I had seen him before, actually, before he started in the NBA. I played against him when he was with Team USA, they were preparing for the Olympics and he was on that Olympic team. I got a call from the Kings—we were in Kansas City at the time—and they told me that the Olympic team was coming through and wanted to play against pro guys. So we ended up playing the game in Lawrence, Kansas. To be perfectly honest, I had not really heard of Michael Jordan much [before then]. We played the game and, I remember calling my brother afterwards and saying, "There is a kid playing on this USA team, I just played against him, and we're going to hear a lot about him in the league." I think I was right, wasn't I?

I just remember how smooth he was on the floor. He was fast, he was quick, and he handled the ball really well. He had a really good-looking jump shot, and he really elevated on it. Basically, it was like, he could get his shot off against anybody. He was playing against pro guys, and he fit right in, he was tough. I was on the team, Reggie King was on the

team, Brook Steppe I think was playing with us. A lot of the old King
It was all pro guys, but he made it look so easy, so I knew we were going
to hear more about him.

From there, it seemed like every time I saw him, he got better and
better. While he was at Carolina, he played within himself and played
within the system, but it was not like he was a household name. You
could not really tell he was going to be great. After he left Carolina, he
got to the pros and started adding facets to his game and just went to
another level. Then he started getting into better and better shape, and
that was a big difference.

When you watched him play, it was like you were just waiting for a
spectacular play. You knew it was coming. Whether it was going to be
a dunk, some play at the rim, it was going to be something. The crowd
knew it. It seemed like it happened every game he played. He got better
and better, and he got better so fast. It seemed like he went from being
a young, raw guy to a great player really fast. He played at a really high
level really early on in his career.

That was noticeable, the way he went from someone trying to fit
into the team and into the league, to someone who was dominating the
league really fast. It was because of how he pushed himself. I remember
talking to Doug Collins when I was working as an assistant for him, he
would tell me stories about coaching Michael when he was coming up
in Chicago. I would talk to him about my days in LA, working with
Kobe Bryant. And it was amazing because there were so many similari-
ties listening to Doug talk about Michael. He hated to lose—even in
practice and scrimmages—he wanted to beat his own teammates. He
was the ultimate competitor.

If they scrimmaged and he lost, he was going to make them play
another game until he won. Losing wasn't an option. I remember
Doug telling me when they would have scrimmages, he would take

ae four guys on the team who were not playing much and he would put Michael on their team and see if Michael could raise their level of competition and confidence against the starters. He refused to lose and was expecting to win.

That's very similar to Kobe. Both were the same way. He was that kind of fierce competitor, just hated to lose. If you beat him, you're going to play another game. He was going to stay until he wins. I saw that drive from Kobe coaching him, and that's the kind of drive that Michael Jordan had, too.[10] Both guys did not need motivation from outside, you didn't need to push them as coaches, they didn't need to read it in the papers—they were just self-driven to be the best. That's how Michael was.

Magic Johnson also recalls how Jordan turned it on for that final game.

It was his game, and he took it over. He could smell the win, and the championship, in the third quarter. We could sense we were done.

When he would start hitting jumpers, he got a feeling of being invincible. He could do the impossible, the unbelievable. But when Michael got it going, his creativity took over, and he started doing things that made us all just shake our heads.

---

[10] Drew was an assistant for the Lakers from 1992–99. Kobe Bryant came into the league in '97.

Tony Smith

Guard

Career: **1991–2001**

Michael Jordan vs. Tony Smith										
Regular Season	**Games**	**Wins**	**Losses**	**Win %**	**Field Goal %**	**PPG**	**Points (High)**	**RPG**	**APG**	**SPG**
Jordan	12	7	5	58.3	50.6	35.6	54 (11/20/92)	6.7	5.0	2.8
Smith	12	5	7	41.7	41.7	4.8	16 (02/23/96)	1.7	1.8	0.7
Playoffs	**Games**	**Wins**	**Losses**	**Win %**	**Field Goal %**	**PPG**	**Points (High)**	**RPG**	**APG**	**SPG**
Jordan	5	5	0	100	45.5	29.6	35 (4/26/96)	4.0	6.2	2.0
Smith	5	0	5	0.0	40.0	6.8	12 (6/12/91	1.0	2.0	1.0

Smith was a long shot to make the NBA as a late second-round pick out of Marquette, but had known Lakers coach Mike Dunleavy from Dunleavy's time in Milwaukee. Given a shot, Smith fashioned a 10-year pro career—and as a rookie, was given the daunting task of dealing with Jordan in the NBA Finals.

I **WAS A ROOKIE;** I was a second-round pick. I had grown up about twenty minutes from Marquette. I played my college basketball, four years, at Marquette, and when I was in college we used to play pickup games against some of the pros; some of the guys who were playing for the Bucks. Mike Dunleavy [Sr.] was one of them, and guys like Phil Pressey. But Mike had come out of retirement with the ucks, and I played with him a few times. So he knew me, he knew my game, and so after my senior year, in 1990, he had just gotten the job coaching the Lakers. He picked me in the second round because he knew my game and knew that, even as a young guy, I was not going to be intimidated.

As a senior at Marquette, I was a scorer and averaged almost 24 points a game.[11] That Lakers team had Magic Johnson, James Worthy, Byron Scott, Sam Perkins. When I got there, I thought, *I am pretty sure they don't need me to score.* So I was trying to figure out how I could get on the floor with a team like that, and I figured it would be as a defensive stopper. That was how I got on the floor all season—if they had somebody tough to guard on the perimeter, that would be my job. They felt confident putting me out there.

In the playoffs, though, rookies don't play as much, and that was the case with me. We had a good team, but it was probably the Bulls' time—Michael Jordan had not yet won one, they had not gotten past the Pistons at that point. It was sort of the end of the great Lakers teams, as everybody was getting older. Jordan was in his prime, Scottie Pippen was getting better, and they had good role players. And then, before Game 5, we were already down 3–1 in the series, we have Byron Scott out and James Worthy out, Worthy had sort of been hurt for most of the series. We had to practice before the game, and we did not even have ten players, so Dunleavy actually got in there and practiced with us.

I had not played much in the series before that.[12] But I knew I was going to have to play more, I was going to get thrown in there. Coach Dunleavy and the veterans on the team, they were not going to come and give me any pep talks. They had seen me throughout the year, they had seen what I was able to do on defense, and they had confidence in me going in, that I was not going to be scared. That was the reason

[11] For his senior year, Smith averaged 23.8 points per game.
[12] Smith had logged just two minutes in the first four games.

Dunleavy put me in, was that he felt I was the best guy on the team to guard him based on what had happened during the regular season. The only thing they told me was, "Play your game." That's it. I remember Magic Johnson telling me and Elden Campbell, who was a rookie, too, "Just go have fun, play hard."

I don't think I was any more or less nervous about that game than I was about any other game I have played, to be honest with you. It was one of those things where, you get into the moment and you're just thinking about competing at that point. You don't even have the time to sit there and think, *Okay, I am going to wind up guarding Michael Jordan here.* You're just thinking what your assignment is and how you want to do it. Of course, it is the toughest assignment on the planet. But I don't think that makes you more nervous or anything, because you're using all your focus to do that and try to do the best job you can. When I look back on it now, it was a fun time and a great opportunity. But I was still a rookie trying to make my way in the league, so being worried about Michael Jordan was definitely not a part of my thought process.

They say Jordan is the toughest cover you could have. It is. I knew that. But with my role on the team, I did not have to worry about scoring. My only real focus was to guard Jordan and make things as difficult as possible on him. Not let him get into his comfort zone and try to get the ball out of his hands. If he scores on you, you have to let it go and just focus on the next time, because you have to realize he scores on everybody. Nobody has ever really shut down Michael Jordan.

He had 30 points in that game. I figure, hey, he had 30 points. That is about as good as the other defenders do on him, right? If Michael Jordan has 30 on you, then I guess that is not too bad. I think he averaged more than that for the series.[13] We actually had a lead late in that game, we were right there with them. Probably the big thing, though, was that he was doing a good job of drawing in the defense and kicking it out. It was John Paxson who really hurt us, in that game and in that

---

[13] Jordan averaged 31.2 points per game during the 1991 Finals.

series. He shot the ball extremely well.[14] So, you could keep Jordan under control a little bit and maybe Scottie Pippen, too, but then if Paxson is making shots, they were really hard to defend.

I don't typically break down my game personally, I just look at it as "Did we win or did we lose?" And we lost. But after the game, some of the guys told me, "You did a good job on him," and most of the points he scored didn't come with me on him, so I can live with that. But I don't really break it down individually, that is for other people to do. It was fun to be part of that, but, I felt like we could have won that game. And we didn't.

Mike Dunleavy Sr. was coach of the Los Angeles Lakers when Michael Jordan finally reached what was then the pinnacle of his success. In 1991, the Bulls defeated the Lakers 4–1 in the best-of-seven NBA finals to give Jordan his first NBA title. Dunleavy remembered the one play in Game 3 that set the Bulls up for victory.

"He made that jump shot over Vlade Divac to tie the game and sent it into overtime," he said. "We were up by 13 and they came back and forced overtime. Jordan's shot put them into overtime with momentum, and that win put them up 2–1. We could not recover.

"The series came down to Michael hitting a tough shot. He had a defender all over him. You can't ask for more than that. There is nobody on earth that can guard Michael Jordan one-on-one."

---

[14] Paxson had 20 points in Game 5 on 9-for-12 shooting.

Jeff Van Gundy

Head Coaching Career: **1996–2007**

Van Gundy was a Knicks assistant coach, first with Stu Jackson and then under Pat Riley from 1989–1996, taking over as the head coach in New York on Riley's departure. He spent five years at the helm in New York, and also coached the Rockets before becoming ESPN's lead analyst.

WE USED TO kiddingly refer to the triangle offense as the "triangle with 23 in the middle." Because Michael was what made [that offense] run. I just went back recently and looked at his numbers. I think sometimes, with great players, you forget just how great they were the longer they're out of the game. I mean, this guy played huge minutes with the Washington Wizards when he was thirty-nine, and averaged 20 points a game. Played all 82 games when he was thirty-eight years old, averaged 22.9 points. Then the run he had with the Bulls, I mean, that was legendary stuff.

But if you don't take a peek back every once in a while, you can start to forget just how great he was.

To me, his post-up game and the triangle offense—how he got into the post, out of the triangle—was the hardest part to guarding him. We didn't have big two-guards at that time in New York, but we did have big point guards. We had Mark Jackson, we had Doc Rivers, and we had Derek Harper. It starts with being a great competitor and having the physical ability; add the two. But we had no answer for him in the post. Defensively it wasn't an every play mentality, but they had the ability— with Michael alongside Scottie Pippen and Horace Grant and Dennis Rodman—to turn it up defensively, such that it was that they could make it very difficult for you to find good shots.

So with Michael Jordan, to me—I don't like to compare eras because I didn't see some of the older guys play live—but with my own two eyes, he was the best. I loved going into Chicago Stadium—the old Chicago Stadium—because you came out of that tunnel, "tunnel three-and-a-half," they called it, and you knew it was on. In a great atmosphere against the greatest to ever play during my time in the NBA. You know, it was an honor to be on the same floor as him and as that team.

I hate to compare players because, ultimately, people will read into it that you're diminishing one player at the expense of the other. I would just say the Bulls team back in their heyday had to go through some monster teams to win it all, some really incredible teams in the Eastern Conference and in the Finals. I think it's hard to compare teams from different eras. But to me, Michael Jordan's Bulls could compete against any of the great teams that ever played. I think they were that good, and they had to go through some great teams to win those championships.

It was unfortunate for us, as he loved playing against New York duing his whole career. In general, he loved the big stage, and Madison Square Garden was that. But he loved competing against a worthy opponent, too, and certainly the teams we put out there were good as a whole, and the competitive nature of the players we had, he saw that as a challenge. Unfortunately, we had our times where we beat him in individual games, but we could never slay the dragon, so to speak. Not in a full playoff series.

They beat us three straight years in the playoffs, 1991, '92, and '93. In '93, we had lost to them in seven games the year before, but had gotten Doc Rivers and Charles Smith in the off-season, and we were a good team. We were in the Conference Finals, had home-court advantage, and had gotten out to a lead by winning the first two games. But they went back [to Chicago] and won Game 3 and then Game 4, which was the big one, as he had 54 points and just took over that game. Then, of course, Game 5, we had a chance to win that down the stretch and that was the Charles Smith game; they blocked his shots in the last few seconds and wound up winning on our home floor, and that was it.[15]

We had great players, and we had tough players. Doc Rivers, Xavier McDaniel, Charles Oakley, who had been his teammate. Anthony Mason. We were tough on him. That's what great competitors want to do. They want to go against the best and be at their best when they do.

Of course, when you're coaching, you'd rather be coaching against a terrible team, because you are just going to worry about everything when you're going against a team like those Bulls teams. You would always like someone who is just oblivious and you can easily beat them. It doesn't happen that way, though. Those Jordan Bulls teams, they played great basketball. From a coaching standpoint, what a challenge that was; trying to come up with ideas to stop that whole team—but mostly to stop Michael Jordan from taking over the whole thing—it was both exhilarating because you were going against greatness and depressing because you didn't have an answer.

---

[15] The Bulls would go on to win Game 6 two days later, 96–88. Jordan would have 25 points, nine assists, two rebounds, three steals, and two blocks.

Jerome Kersey

Forward

Career: 1985–2001
Career Highlights: .... 1999 NBA Finals Champion

Michael Jordan vs. Jerome Kersey										
Regular Season	Games	Wins	Losses	Win %	Field Goal %	PPG	Points (High)	RPG	APG	SPG
Jordan	19	12	7	63.1	47.8	34.2	53 (1/8/87)	6.9	6.5	2.6
Kersey	19	7	12	36.9	35.8	10.4	21 (11/21/91)	6.4	2.1	1.3
Playoffs	Games	Wins	Losses	Win %	Field Goal %	PPG	Points (High)	RPG	APG	SPG
Jordan	6	4	2	66.7	52.6	35.8	46 (6/12/92)	4.8	6.5	1.7
Kersey	6	2	4	33.3	48.1	14.8	24 (6/14/92)	8.7	3.3	1.8

Coming out of tiny Longwood University, Kersey was overlooked in the 1984 draft, but wound up with Portland, and stuck there for 11 of his 17 NBA seasons. He gained prominence going against Jordan in the 1987 Slam Dunk contest and would later face Jordan in a much more crucial stage—the 1992 NBA Finals.

I **WAS PART OF** that 1984 draft, too, the one where the Blazers took Sam Bowie instead of Michael Jordan with the second pick. I was not quite the big name as him or some of those guys—I had gone to Longwood in North Carolina, and I was the 46th pick in that draft. Not many people really knew about me. But that was ACC country, so I watched all of those games, no question, and North Carolina was a great team at that time.

I always defend what the Blazers did in that draft. I know it looks a certain way now, but at the time it made sense. I mention to people all the time, the year before they drafted Clyde Drexler, and they had Jim Paxson, and he was good. Jim Paxson was All-Pro. Calvin Natt was the starter at small forward, so the year before Clyde was not even a starter. Before that draft, they traded Calvin Natt and they got Kiki Vandeweghe, and he was an All-Star. You had Jim Paxson, Kiki Vandeweghe, and Clyde Drexler, all at the 2 and 3 spots. They couldn't duplicate the same position again, when they had Clyde there and he was not even a starter.

They needed a center, and Sam Bowie was the most viable center available at that point, Hakeem Olajuwon was the first pick. What were you going to do? In the structure of that team, how were you going to take another guard? There wasn't a need for another two-guard at that point. No one knew at the time just how good Michael Jordan was going to be.

We played against each other a few times over the years, no question about that. But probably the first time we went head-to-head was the Slam Dunk contest in 1987.

The thing is, I was a substitute that year. Dominique Wilkins was supposed to be the guy, and everyone was hoping to see those two go against each other again. And if you watch it now, I actually thought Terrence Stansbury was the one who should have been in the finals. He had the Statue of Liberty deal, he could make the 360-degree dunks, and it was in Seattle, he was playing for the Sonics. He was the home-town guy. I thought he would be in the final, but he got a couple of tough scores from the judges and did not make it. He probably deserved it.

For me, I am a power dunker. I am not a finesse kind of dunker, I don't have huge hands like Michael. But I just tried to go out and do what I could do and finish it with power. Michael's dunks all have a lot of finesse to them because he hangs in the air and is able to do all these things with moving his body, legs, and feet in different angles. So I was watching him and, I thought I had a chance, but you watch him and you can't help but think, *Oh, that is going to be tough to beat.* He did the foul-line dunk, he ran the length of the court and took off and put it through. He had the one on the baseline where he almost looked like he was horizontal when he was going in. How do you top that?

I was there, though, I had some good dunks. But by the time the final came, honestly, I was not thinking I would still be dunking at that point. I did not think that I would make it that far, so I really didn't have anything planned. I kind of ran out of material. My best dunks are the ones that come in the flow of a game, on people, in transition—situational dunks. It is not showy like Michael's are with the big hands and the tongue wagging and all that stuff. But I gave my best showing. It was going to be hard to beat Michael at that point. I made it close, and I am happy about that.[16]

We had some good battles in the regular season over the years. You were not going to stop him altogether, but I always tried to play him tough, and I think I was able to. So, when the Finals came around in 1992, the goal going into those games was to just try and make him play in a crowd, make him see bodies in front of him. That was the game plan that Rick [Adelman] drew up for us. We were a smart team, a veteran team. And we were similar to them. Clyde Drexler was our big scorer, he averaged 25 points or so, but we had a lot of really good role players around him—Terry Porter, Kevin Duckworth, Buck Williams, Cliff Robinson. We could get up and down and score a lot, but we were a very good defensive team, too, and lot of people overlooked that.

If you go back, the year before, the Bulls beat the Lakers to win their first championship, and they were more confident the next year. They had gotten through those battles with the Pistons, and they had Scottie

---

[16] Kersey finished with 140 points in the final round, while Jordan had 146.

Pippen coming into his own; he was in his fourth year or so himself. He gained that confidence, Michael had gotten him to the point where he showed him he could be a star in the league. Then they had guys around them like Bill Cartwright and Steve Kerr and John Paxson—these guys were really good veteran players. Michael was the star, but they had guys who knew their roles, and everybody did what they were supposed to on that team. So you could not just focus on Michael Jordan, because they had other ways to beat you, too. It was their team.

The thing about championship games are, there are only one or two plays that can change some of these games. And when they are closely contested, that can make all the difference in whether you win or lose. I thought the year that the Bulls beat the Lakers, that might have been our best team. We were 63–19 that year and just had a great season, but we got into the playoffs and lost to the Lakers in the Western Conference Finals. We lost the first game of that series at home, and that erased the home-court advantage right there. We went on to lose that series, and the Bulls beat the Lakers in the Finals for the championship.

We started that year off, we had won 19 of 20 games to begin the year, and we had actually handled Chicago pretty well both times we played them. We beat them at our place by double-digits; Clyde had a really big game.[17] I later talked to B. J. Armstrong about it when we played together in Golden State. He told me, "Man, we were so glad the Lakers beat you guys, we did not want to play you in the Finals that year."

But we did not get past the Lakers, and so we did not get to face the Bulls in the Finals until the next year. For the most part, I thought we did a pretty good job executing our game plan. The first game, he hit all the 3s, but he was on the outside. Michael was not known as a prolific 3-point shooter, so those were the shots we wanted him to take . . . he just happened to catch fire that night for some reason. You want him

---

[17] Drexler scored 30 points with seven rebounds and nine assists when Portland defeated Chicago at home, 125–112, on November 18, 1990.

to be on the outside and not attacking, attacking, attacking, creating shots for himself and the guys around him. We did a good job having bodies around him and trying to make it as difficult as possible. He was so good, though, that you could execute the game plan just right, but he might still make the shots. That's what happened in that series.

That Game 6 was a tough one, because we had a big lead there.[18] We had a lot of careless turnovers in that game. I had one at half court. We had a couple in the backcourt, and they got points off those—I think Bob Hansen, one of their bench guys who did not even play much the whole series, he hit a 3 out of the corner on the left side on one of those plays. That was big for them. Their bench players came in and kind of started scrapping and rushed us a little bit. We were playing like we were just trying to hold the lead and end the game so we could get to Game 7. We stopped doing what got us the lead in the first place. When you do that, you make mistakes.

Their bench guys were playing like they had nothing to lose . . . and really they didn't. Before you knew it, they were back close to us and had a shot at [winning] again. They took that momentum and kept going to win the game. Those careless turnovers add up against a team like those Bulls, and you get some calls going against you here and there. Everything changes fast in a series like that. That's the way the game goes, though. I would have liked to have seen what would have happened in Game 7.

For me, individually, guarding Michael Jordan was as hard as anything you could do on the court. I think there are a few things you can't give him. First, you can't give him the jump shot. Second, you can't give him the right hand. You probably want to push him to his left if you can—ideally, you don't let him go either way, you stay in front of him.

---

[18] Portland led by a score of 79–64 heading into the fourth quarter.

You don't want to give him a lane to the middle where he can break y
defense down.

I was bigger than Michael, I was taller and bigger.[19] So that is what
I tried to do, to get him out of his comfort zone. I tried to be real
physical and push him to his left as much as possible so that then he
is fading away from the basket and not going toward the basket. It
worked sometimes. Sometimes it didn't. With a great player like that,
sometimes, you just have to live with what he is going to get. If the star
is going to get enough shots, he is going to make a lot of them. You just
don't want them to be easy ones.

If he is not the greatest player in NBA history, he is one of the top
two or three, definitely. No matter what you do on defense, it might
not matter. He has proved what he can do out on the court, so you
have to take your hat off to him.

---

[19] Kersey was listed at 6-7, 215 pounds. Jordan was 6-6, 195.

Terry Porter

Forward

NBA Career: 1986–2002
Head Coaching Career: 2004–05, 2009
Career Highlights: ....two-time NBA All-Star

Michael Jordan vs. Terry Porter										
Regular Season	Games	Wins	Losses	Win %	Field Goal %	PPG	Points (High)	RPG	APG	SPG
Jordan	21	14	7	66.7	50.5	34.8	53 (1/8/87)	6.3	5.7	2.0
Porter	21	7	14	33.3	45.6	12.8	25 (12/8/90)	3.0	7.4	1.3

Playoffs	Games	Wins	Losses	Win %	Field Goal %	PPG	Points (High)	RPG	APG	SPG
Jordan	6	4	2	66.7	52.6	35.8	46 (6/12/92)	4.8	6.5	1.7
Porter	6	2	4	33.3	47.1	16.2	24 (6/5/92)	4.3	4.7	1.0

Porter was drafted the same year as Michael Jordan and played against him numerous times while with the Portland Trail Blazers, Minnesota Timberwolves, Miami Heat, and San Antonio Spurs. He was the starting point guard for the Portland Trail Blazers that played the Bulls in the 1992 NBA Finals. Porter eventually went on to coaching—and twice was a head coach—once with Milwaukee and once with Phoenix.

O BVIOUSLY, I REMEMBER the 1992 NBA Finals when I played against him with the Portland Trail Blazers. That was my least favorite moment playing against him. He was an unbelievable competitor. Because I was in the West, I only got to see him twice a year. I remember in the 1990–91 season, we played them twice and beat them by ⌐ both times, and there was a lot of talk that we were going to meet them in the Finals that year, so there was always an undercurrent of story lines when we played. We really wanted to meet them in the Finals that year, but we lost to the Lakers in the Western Conference Finals. We thought we could beat the Bulls. It would have been interesting to see what might have happened.

In the '92 Finals, the one thing that sticks out was his ability to knock down the 3-point shot in that one game. Coming into the series he had been shooting something like 20 percent, but he ended up making four out of five in that game and he did that shrug. So many moments he was famous for, and I guess it is cool that I was involved in one of them. We played them six games in that series, and his ability to hit the big shot was the big difference.

I didn't guard him that much, Clyde [Drexler] guarded him, but when did I guard him, he would just call for the ball and shoot it over me. There wasn't that much talking between us. But you heard him talking all the time to Clyde. They had some great battles.

You were always excited about playing him. He and his team were one of the best teams in the league at the time, and now one of the best teams in history.

Tim Kempton

Forward

Career: **1987–1998**

Michael Jordan vs. Tim Kempton										
Regular Season	Games	Wins	Losses	Win %	Field Goal %	PPG	Points (High)	RPG	APG	SPG
Jordan	10	8	2	80.0	55.9	30.6	40 (twice)	6.1	6.9	2.8
Kempton	10	2	8	20.0	57.1	5.0	16 (12/23/88)	3.5	0.9	0.2

Kempton, a sixth-round pick out of Notre Dame, holds the almost unique distinction of never having played for the same NBA teams two consecutive years, remarkable considering he did play for eight NBA seasons. He managed to latch on with the Suns in 1992–93, and was part of the Phoenix team that reached the NBA Finals.

I THINK BECAUSE CHICAGO was so dominant and so good at that time, the teams that comes up short are kind of an afterthought. People don't think about how good our team was, though. Obviously, Charles Barkley was the dominant personality, he had come from Philadelphia that year and was the MVP. He was just outstanding. Leaving Philadelphia and getting a better supporting cast around him, he really approached that season as a big chance for him to finally win a ring. We had Tom Chambers, even though he was at the end of his career, he was part of that team and he was still a prominent player. Kevin Johnson, Dan Majerle, Danny Ainge, Cedric Ceballos— it was an exceptional bunch of guys. Everybody respected everyone else because they understood the roles they were playing. And Paul Westphal was probably the perfect coach for that team.

It was a strange series because they came to our building and won two games, we were close in Game 2, but we had a last-second shot blocked. We went to Chicago and won two out of three there. Then they came back and beat us in Phoenix again, clinching the series on our floor. They won three games on our home floor. That is really hard to do.

I think it was a little bit that we kind of got blindsided in those first two games, with them winning in Phoenix. To be honest, I think there was a little bit of gamesmanship by Michael Jordan with Charles. They were close, they were good friends—but they were going out all the time—before the series started and even during the series, playing golf, all of that. Michael had already won it. He knew what it took. There was a lot that went on that was like, "Oh, no. Chuck and Michael were out again last night." Or, "Chuck and Mike were at the Biltmore [Hotel] again." But it was not being broadcast, not many people were talking about it in the open.

We lost those first two games, we went to Chicago and we started to get our rhythm back. It was probably good for us to get out of Phoenix and get focused. There was a lot of disappointment, kind of a deer-in-the-headlights sort of thing, us saying, "What the hell just happened?" We were 62–20, we won a tough series against Seattle in the Western Conference Finals, we were rolling. It was definitely good to get out of Phoenix after those first two games, but I was surprised just because I was around it and knowing what was going on, Charles and Michael were not really talked about. You know, maybe Charles should have waited till after the series to hang out with Michael. But getting to Chicago, we went and we won Game 3, the triple-overtime game, one of the greatest games in the Finals, and we started feeling like we were back in it.

Game 4 of that series, Michael was just incredible. He was going to the basket, over and over, and we tried everything on him. Paul Westphal used every option he had—Kevin Johnson, Richard Dumas, [Dan] Majerle. Nothing worked, Michael just kept coming. There was a play at the end of the half, he just did a hesitation dribble, got by Majerle, and absolutely flew in—really high—for the dunk. I remember going into the locker room at halftime of that Game 4, and the coaches were saying, "Listen, Michael is locked in. He might get 60. Let's concentrate on the other guys and see what we can do as far as limiting them. We can't have the other guys step up have good nights when Michael has it going like that, when he is locked in." We knew he was not going to score 100 points, so we had be sure the other players on that team were not going to hurt us, too.

We actually did a pretty good job of it. We were down by double digits in the second half,[20] but we had a comeback and we were even in the fourth quarter. But down the stretch, it was just more of Michael. He was too much. We were down two points near the end of the game, and he kind of went in for a little floater, got fouled, and that was it.[21] We felt like we had a chance to even up that series, but Michael was just too much that night.

The end of that Game 6, everybody remembers John Paxson hitting the big shot,[22] but we really hit a wall at the end of that game. And by that, I mean, we ran into that defense of theirs. That was such an underrated strength of those Chicago teams, with Michael, with Scottie—to be able to lock in defensively. They were so good at it. When they needed one or two stops late in a game, they were going to

---

[20] Phoenix trailed by 13 in the third quarter.

[21] With Chicago ahead, 106–104, Jordan made a 6-footer with 13.3 second to play and drew a foul on Barkley. After he made the free throw, the Bulls led by five.

[22] Paxson won the game and the series by making a 3-pointer with 3.9 seconds on the clock to give Chicago a 99–98 lead.

get it, whether it was Michael on the perimeter or Scottie, with those guys behind them.

That is what it seemed like at the end there, when we just needed one bucket to keep it going and get a little separation, get back into our rhythm. Anything. It was just not there.[23] That was what Chicago's strength really was. We were saying, "Can't we just score one bucket and we'll be all right?" They had the ability to say, "No, no you can't." That's how good their defense was. Every once in a while with great teams, you see that one thing that they do better than anyone else, and I thought with the Bulls, it was their ability to get a stop when they wanted it. We were an explosive offensive team at that time, we scored a lot of points in that postseason, but at the end of Game 6, it just seemed like no one could get it going. So you have to give them credit for that.

---

[23] Phoenix led 98–94 with 2:23 to play but failed to score again in the game.

Mark West

Center

Career: **1984–2000**

Michael Jordan vs. Mark West										
Regular Season	Games	Wins	Losses	Win %	Field Goal %	PPG	Points (High)	RPG	APG	SPG
Jordan	34	22	12	64.7	51.5	33.6	53 (1/21/89, 3/7/96)	5.9	5.3	2.4
West	34	12	22	35.3	60.0	5.4	18 (4/12/95)	4.7	0.5	0.3

Playoffs	Games	Wins	Losses	Win %	Field Goal %	PPG	Points (High)	RPG	APG	SPG
Jordan	7	5	2	71.4	51.6	39.3	55 (6/16/93)	8.9	6.0	1.6
West	7	2	5	28.6	63.6	5.1	11 (6/13/93)	3.9	0.6	0.0

West was a 6-10 center and a reliable veteran who stayed in the NBA for 17 seasons. His best years, though, came with Phoenix, and he was a key cog off the bench for the Suns team that reached the 1993 NBA Finals.

WE HAD A good team, we had Charles Barkley in his first year there, we had Kevin Johnson, we still had Tom Chambers, and we had Dan Majerle. Charles was in great shape, he really wanted to win, and he had a great cast of players around him. We won 62 games that year, and as a matter of fact, we had home-court advantage throughout the playoffs, too. That was big because we had some tough series in the West, getting through the Sonics especially; they were a really good team.

We did not have experience, though, in those Finals. That's what the Bulls had over us, and that made a big difference.

We came in and lost those first two games at home, and that was a hard pill to swallow. We were sort of set back on our heels. I don't think any one of us expected them to come into our building and win both games. We came back and played much better in Chicago—we won two in Chicago, we should have won three—but you are not going to win a series against a team like that if you can't win one on your home court. We got back to Phoenix for that Game 6 and were pretty confident; we still thought we had a chance to win the series. We were up in that Game 6, but we got cold at the end, their defense was really good, and the last-second shot by John Paxson sealed the deal for us.

I thought Game 3 was one of the best games I've been part of. Kevin Johnson struggled in Game 2, but he got put onto Michael in Game 3, and the strategy was pretty clear: just keep Michael in front of him, so that he was not attacking the basket and getting to the free-throw line and getting fouls called on our big guys in the interior. Kevin did a great job making him shoot jumpers, making him go to that baseline jumper and making him shoot pull-ups. Sometimes you could do that and Jordan was going to make them anyway. But in that Game 3, they were not going down for the most part, and Kevin was doing a good job on him defensively that way. That gave us an opportunity to work on everybody else. It worked, and we won the game in double over-time. It was a difficult game but we gave ourselves a chance to get back into the series.

Michael was going to score, and we knew that. You always wanted to make it difficult for him to get his points, see if you could get him to miss some shots. But you were not going to win that battle every time. So it becomes, if I can't win that one, which battles can we win? Can we win the battle of bench players? Can we win the battle in the middle? Can we win something that gives us a chance? We could find places we could win—we had Chuck at forward, we knew we could win that one, we had Kevin Johnson at point guard, but they did a really good job with him and having all their guns loaded with guys like B. J. Armstrong and that crew. We had some advantages, and that is why we had a shot to win that series.

I *do* think not having Cedric Ceballos hurt us. He would have been another guy who would have occupied Scottie Pippen. Cedric could score, and he would have been another guy who, defensively, would have given us some help. It is hard playing against a team like that without all your bullets—it is hard enough with all your players healthy. I am not necessarily saying that we would have won if this guy was healthy or that guy was healthy, it just gives you more of a chance to deal with them.

Game 4, the way Jordan played, scoring 55 points, it was pretty incredible. I had seen something like that before. I had seen Tom score 60 in Seattle,[24] and you know sometimes a guy just gets in that mode, I had seen that before. I just always hoped I would not be on the wrong end of one, and especially not in the NBA Finals like that. It was early on in the game when, you're watching him and the way he was attacking the basket and at a certain point in time, you just think, *You're not going to stop him, he is rolling.* So it became a matter of trying to close down the avenues for their other scorers, attacking them that way. At the end of the day, you were not just trying to beat Michael Jordan, you were trying to beat the Bulls. If he was going to score, don't let the other guys score, too.

But they were a great team, and that was really when those guys—Michael and Charles—were at their best. It was really a great series to be part of, but the frustrating part is, when you think about certain things that happened, when you think about the little things that changed the series, you can't help but think we at least had a chance to win that one.

---

[24] Chambers set a Suns record with 60 points against the Sonics, his old team, on March 24, 1990.

Paul Westphal

NBA Career: 1973–84
Head Coaching Career: 1993–96, 1999–2001, 2010–2012
Career Highlights: .... five-time All-Star, 1974 NBA Finals
Champion

As a player, Westphal was a five-time All-Star who played in the Finals twice and won one championship. As a coach, he was on an NBA sideline for 10 seasons, compiling a record of 318–279. In 1992–93, he had just taken over for Suns icon Cotton Fitzsimmons, and his 62–20 record that year was the best of his coaching career.

WHAT STOOD OUT to me at that time was just how much the NBA had grown. I had been involved in the NBA pretty much my entire adult life. I had played in the Finals before. I can remember when the Celtics and the Bucks were in the Finals, my second year in the league (in 1974), that was a fantastic series also—you had John Havlicek and Dave Cowens, Kareem Abdul-Jabbar and Oscar Robertson, it was a seven-game series, and it was a great, great series in a lot of ways. But the press, there were maybe two or three beat writers at the games, and some of the writers from New York would come. But it was like the regular season, only a little bigger.

By the time we played the Bulls in 1993, though, they had to hold a press conference on the practice floor at the America West Arena, and it was jammed. That was a credit to the personalities in that series, but especially Michael Jordan. He had become someone who just drew in so much interest from all over the world. A lot of reporters could not get into those practice press conferences. You couldn't turn around in there; there was so much press, from all over the globe. There were helicopters following Charles [Barkley] around, whenever he played golf. The magnitude of how the game had grown is what hit me the most. It was just after the Dream Team summer, so it was huge. It was truly a global thing.

We lost the first two games of the series in Phoenix, but I wouldn't say that we were not ready for that stage or anything like that. I think we were ready, we were well-prepared, we had gone through the Western Conference playoffs. We knew what it took to win. Our team had confidence. We were prepared, but we just ran up against a team that had good games. In the Finals, people tend to see them as a group of games, but they're each an individual game; each game has its own personality. We just lost the first two games.

We came back after those first two and won the next one in triple overtime on their home floor. It was just a hard-fought game; Chicago was a tough place to play. But we felt that we could win any time we played, anywhere we played. I am sure the Bulls felt the same way. But we had just lost the first two on our home floor, and we knew what the challenge ahead of us was going to be. So we showed up and fought our hardest and managed to win the game on their home floor. We never thought it was going to be easy. That got us back into it.

I do remember that Kevin [Johnson] had a horrible game in Phoenix in Game 2.[25] And people were all over him: the fans, the media,

---

[25] Johnson fouled out in thirty-two minutes, scoring four points and committing four turnovers.

everyone. But Charles came in and went to his defense in a big way; he was not going to pile on him. Charles came out and said, "He is my teammate, I believe in him, we are going to come back and be better." I always thought that was something Kevin appreciated.

After that, Kevin took on the responsibility of guarding Michael Jordan in Game 3. And he did it for sixty-three minutes. There was a story, in fact, that I told Kevin he would guard Jordan, then he fell asleep on the team plane and woke up and said, "Coach, I had a nightmare that you told me I was going to guard Michael Jordan." But he was kidding. He wanted that responsibility, he was not afraid of that challenge. And he did it for all that time, right through triple overtime, and we won the game. I was so proud of both Kevin and Charles for what they showed as far as togetherness and grit, having that championship DNA. It was great to see and to be a part of.

We tried everything against Jordan in that series. We went through everything we had in the playbook. We would try to double-team him. Sometimes we wouldn't, we would leave him one-on-one. Sometimes we would send help late on certain areas of the floor. We tried to put Dan Majerle on him. We put Kevin on him—he gave up a lot of size—but we just needed to give him different looks as much as we could. In that triple-overtime game, Kevin played just about every second of that game. I took him out for a few seconds at the end of one of the quarters, and that was the only time he was not on the floor. So that works out to just about sixty-three minutes, and in that game, Kevin was on Michael for all sixty-three of those minutes, or however long Michael was out there. He scored a lot, but Kevin did a good job making him work for those points.[26] Nobody ever stopped him and we didn't either. But we tried to make him work.

Game 4, he scored 55 points, and we threw everything we had at him. Nothing worked, though. It was a magnificent performance, no

---

[26] Jordan played fifty-seven minutes in Game 3, and though he had 44 points, he was just 19-for-43 (44.1%) shooting.

doubt about it, he was very aggressive and came out attacking right from the beginning. There is a lot that went into him carrying them in that game and in that series. They had a great team, we had a great team. I always say, if those two teams played a hundred times, we would win fifty and they would win fifty. But I think you have to acknowledge how magnificent Michael Jordan was in that series. You have got to give the guy credit.

Jim Cleamons

NBA Career:	1972–80
Head Coaching Career:	1997–98
Career Highlights:	1972 NBA Finals Champion

Cleamons played nine years in the NBA, and among his teammates was Phil Jackson with the Knicks in the late 1970s. When Jackson was named head coach of the Bulls, he called on Cleamons to be one of his assistants, and Cleamons was with Chicago from 1989–1996.

MICHAEL WAS JUST a hard worker. That's the most basic thing that you can't overlook and what probably does get overlooked too much. He had a passion, a desire for the game that has been rarely seen and seldom exhibited in this business, certainly not at his level. His competitiveness, his drive, his will to improve, it was uncanny. As a teacher, you're happy to have someone like that who accepted the importance of coming to work on a daily basis and always wanting to put in a good effort for a good day's pay.

I came in with the group of coaches that came in for the 1989–90 season,[27] and some of the groundwork of what made him so good had already been laid. All of us coaches in that group were the beneficiaries of the fact that he wanted to win so badly. The Bulls teams that came before us had been good, really good. But their inability to achieve in certain areas laid that groundwork for that desire, both for Michael and the overall group. They'd gotten to a certain level, but their competitiveness was already being challenged—they had lost in the playoffs a couple of times already, to the Pistons, so they were already pretty frustrated by that.[28]

As the stars began to align with the system that Phil brought with him and the other coaches we had—primarily Johnny Bach and Tex Winter—the players got a better sense of how we wanted the team to grow. When you combined that with the team's desire to achieve and move forward, it all became very instinctual. It was easy for me to relate to them, as a coach and former player. And for them, they *bought in*, as they say in the vernacular now, because they were ready to improve. They had the desire, there was a change in leadership with the coaching staff, and it was just time for them to say, "Okay, we have been doing things one way, now we have to be willing to accept a different voice, a different philosophy." They were tired of beating their heads against the wall.

There was a lot of work to do, but it was not like you had to go in and beg them—they were willing to accept what we were trying to get them to do. That started with Michael. When your best player—and obviously Michael was the best player—leads by example like that, the other leaders of the team start following and start speaking up about his example as a player. A lot of times in the NBA, your best player might kind of dog it in practice; kind of do what he wants to do. A lot of teams deal with that. But here was a young player, who was, in every

---

[27] The season in which Phil Jackson took over for Doug Collins.
[28] The Bulls fell to the Pistons five games in the Conference Semifinals in 1988, and in six games in the Eastern Conference Finals in '89.

area, giving you maximum effort. He is competitive, he is challeng
his teammates to be competitive and play hard along with him.

I had come from the collegiate level,[29] where you are the authority
and guys are willing to work and listen and buy in because you're the
coach and they need you. But at the professional level, players can be
really jaded. They come to practice because it is required of them and
they don't give you the competitiveness in practice that they save for
the game. And so you just hope that what you see at game time is a
certain level of competitiveness.

But when you have a guy like Michael, who got his team to really
work in practice, the results of those practices foreshadow what you
were going to get in the game. He approached practice as a time
to work just as hard as you do in a game. If you are going hard in
practice, you are playing against the guy every day. You know what
his favorite move is; you know where he is going to go to get his
shot off. You know the tricks he is going to use. But when you are
playing a team—even a conference rival—they might now some of
what you do from the scouting report, but they are not going to
know as much as the one who sees you every day in practice. So
you go deeper into the bag of tricks, you develop more and more
parts of your game, other skills. That is what would happen with
Michael. He would challenge his teammates to take away his go-to
moves, and that way he would develop more moves.

He developed trust, too. That is a very important aspect of what
happened when we got there. We had to get everyone on that team to
trust each other, even Michael. I go back to our championship we won
in the first series against the Lakers.[30] In the last game of that series—
Michael had been phenomenal in the series—he was over 30 points
per game,[31] the Lakers had gotten the score close in the fourth quarter.

---

[29] Cleamons was the head coach at Youngstown State in Ohio from 1988–89.

[30] In 1991, which was the Bulls' first championship.

[31] He averaged 31.2 points, with 11.4 assists per game.

down the stretch, over the last five minutes or so, we kept running the same play—fourth quarter, Michael kept hitting John Paxson for open looks. Three, maybe four times in a row. The defense was sucked into Michael, and Pax was the open guy. He did not hesitate to find Pax each one of those times. The ego that gets in the way sometimes is, "Well, hell, I can make this shot." But the preaching from our coaches was to hit the open man, and Pax was the open man. So rather than Michael force three, four shots, whatever it was—it was the same scenario, almost, each time, bam, bam, bam—he let Pax shoot it and let Pax earn his trust. And Pax knocked them all down. Michael understood the formula. From that, from that 1990–91 championship, he understood and once he got it, he did not deviate. He did not need to wonder whether it was going to work, he understood it.

That set in motion the bigger legacy. He did not try to change it. He had his games with 45, 50. He averaged 30 points and all. But he won three championships in a row. He left, retired, came back, and won three more. Because he understood the formula, he believed it. That's true greatness.

You saw it in the following year, too, when we got to the Finals again and beat Portland. I think what happened, when you initially have that breakthrough, you become team-oriented, so that you know that each other's performance relies on yourself and on the next individual. You begin to see the benefits of that labor and the discipline that goes into it. Their expectations with each other changed, they began to trust each other more and have faith that if you do your job and your assignment, the other guys are going to do the same.

If you go back and look, we were in the Finals against Portland in 1992. It was Game 6, the final game of the series. Midway through the third quarter, we were down and by the end of the third, we were behind maybe 15 points.[32] Phil pulled out the starters and put the

---

[32] The Bulls were trailing at the end of the third quarter, 79–64.

reserves out there with Scottie Pippen.[33] They got on a roll, got things going, and they cut that lead down—they're the ones who got it done. We had given up the ghost, we were thinking, *Okay, this thing is going another game.*

But then the bench got going and the starters were cheering them on, everyone was into it. Portland started to get a little shaky, you could sense it. They were not prepared for this from our bench guys. From the end of that third quarter going to about halfway into the fourth, the bench brought us back and got us to three points down; put us in position to win that game.

Michael went back into the game about halfway through the fourth, and of course, you know what happened. We forced some turnovers down the stretch and came back. We wound up winning that sucker right there. But it was because of the bench.

As a teacher—and if you are a coach, you are a teacher first—you respected Michael because he allowed you to do your job. That tells you a lot about a person. He could have very easily brushed you off or, once you start talking, he could give you the roll of the eyes or take the attitude of, "I have heard this before, what do you know?" And if he does that, it sets the tone for the team and makes your job harder, makes it harder to just teach. But we won games and we won series because of the way he approached it, his willingness to let us teach. It helped us teach not only him, but the guys on the bench, the guys who won us that game against Portland.

When you have a person in the classroom who is an A student and, because they are an A student, they don't respect the other students who are maybe struggling a little more with math or chemistry or whatever it may be, you just want that student to have enough to respect for the environment to say, "Hey, maybe I can learn something, too." You appreciate that, out of his humanity and respect of himself and others,

---

[33] On the floor with Pippen were Stacey King, Scott Williams, Bob Hansen, and B. J. Armstrong.

just because he was a good player he did not put himself above the group. He still wanted you to help him be a better player.

As much as what was going on around him with the commercials and the magazines, he never lost that "Yeah, I am a good player, but there is a lot more I can learn from this game." He got a lot out of it, allowed himself to be coached and see how the pieces fit together. There is no arguing with the results.

Section Three: At the Top

"It was like they were the future Hall of Famers that they were, and us, we were like a ninth grade girls' team."

—Former Indiana Pacer, Jalen Rose

MICHAEL JORDAN STUNNED the sports world when he announced that he would retire from the Bulls and the NBA after the 1993 season to pursue a career in baseball. He had just turned thirty at the time, had won his third straight championship and his seventh straight scoring title. Never before had an athlete at the top of his game in a major American team sport simply decided to go off and pick up another major American sport.

After two years dabbling in baseball, Jordan returned to the Bulls near the end of the 1995 season, playing the final 17 games with the team. He was not in peak basketball shape, though, and struggled down the stretch of the season—he averaged 26.9 points on just 41.1 percent shooting—with the Bulls ultimately eliminated from the play-offs in the Eastern Conference Semifinals by the Magic in six games.

The following year, though, Jordan arrived in camp completely back in basketball condition, and the rest of the Bulls—bolstered by the arrival of eccentric rebounding machine Dennis Rodman—were also at their peak. The 1995–96 Bulls got off to a 41–3 start and wound up breaking the league's regular-season win record, with 72, cruising through the playoffs to the NBA championship with a 15–3 postseason record.

It was during this time that Jordan and the Bulls achieved their most consistent success, going 203–43 and winning three more consecutive titles. In this section, players and coaches discuss the difficulty of dealing with defending Jordan and those top-shelf Bulls teams of the 1990s.

Jalen Rose

Guard/Forward

Career: 1995–2007
Career Highlights: .... **2000 Most Improved Player**

Michael Jordan vs. Jalen Rose										
Regular Season	Games	Wins	Losses	Win %	Field Goal %	PPG	Points (High)	RPG	APG	SPG
Jordan	15	10	5	66.7	44.2	23.1	38 (3/7/97)	5.3	4.4	1.7
Rose	15	5	10	33.3	44.1	13.9	27 (2/3/02)	3.3	3.5	0.9

Playoffs	Games	Wins	Losses	Win %	Field Goal %	PPG	Points (High)	RPG	APG	SPG
Jordan	6	3	3	50.0	44.9	44.9	41 (5/19/98)	5.5	4.2	1.8
Rose	6	3	3	50.0	47.5	7.8	15 (5/23/98)	2.3	2.2	0.3

A part of the famed Michigan "Fab Five," Rose played for six teams over 13 seasons in the NBA, but had his best years in Indiana in the late 1990s. He averaged more than 20 points per game in three different seasons, and was part of the Pacers team that lost to the Bulls in a stunning seventh-game collapse in the 1998 Eastern Conference Finals.

MICHAEL JORDAN, TO me, it is like a tale of two—or well, actually, a tale of three MJs for me.

I grew up in Detroit, a Detroit native, so I was a Pistons fan. At that time, I never truly got a chance to appreciate the greatness of some of the players of that time—his greatness and Larry Bird's greatness in particular—because they were our rivals. They were the Pistons' rivals. And I rooted against them so much for so many years that it clouded my judgment about how great he was, to be honest with you.

111

I remember at that time, it was the discussion of who is the best as a scorer between Michael Jordan, who was the big scorer, and Dominique Wilkins, who was also the big scorer. But that was before Phil Jackson and Horace Grant and Scottie Pippen came along, and then everything changed. Then he obviously went on to become a great, six-time champion. But first, he was just this pure scorer.

And during that period, I was on the Pacers. We were playing against him in '98 in the playoffs, his last year [before his first retirement]. We took him and the Bulls to Game 7 in the Eastern Conference Finals that year. If I had to refer to a scenario that really stands out about him, it would be that Game 7. We were beating them by 17 points in Game 7 in Chicago, and we had a chance to get to the NBA Finals.

All of a sudden it changed, and he and Scottie Pippen just turned up the defense. It was like they were the future Hall of Famers that they were, and us, we were like a ninth grade girls' team. That's what it was like, the way they just took the ball away from us with their defense. Not to show disrespect toward us in any way, shape, or form, but that's how great he was, and they were. He was clutch; he was the best clutch player I've [ever] seen. It showed in that series.

And I think it was his competitive spirit that made the difference. It was his will to win. He was almost always the best player on the floor, not only on the offensive end but also on the defensive end. He imposed his will and leadership on the other players. He could play you in the post, he had strong hands, and as he got older he developed into a great outside shooter and a great 3-point shooter. That's why he became the black cat and the greatest player of all time.

My last memory of Jordan was the comeback with Washington. Yeah, he was definitely Superman in his prime, but now I'm coming into my prime, and we (the Bulls) are playing against the Wizards. So of course, I'm going to see if I can turn him back into Clark Kent.

I was playing in Chicago for the Bulls a couple of times when his return happened, and in that situation, I was really trying to go at him. [In one game I dunked on him. Actually,] I didn't so much dunk on him as I did around him, but I came down off the rim and started talking trash. I did that a lot, and Jordan always brought it out in me. I said something rude and disrespectful, and got ejected. We were playing on national TV. I could have had the game of my life if I could have stayed in the game. That was stupid.

But, by the way, he was still averaging 20 points a game, basically, the only All-Star on that team, and he was the only guy on their team at his age to play all 82 games.[1] So I have a terrific amount of respect for him; for the way he came back and was able to play so well at that age. He wasn't the same, but he was still very good.

But, even though he was older, I admit, I did feel good about one time playing for Chicago against his Wizards, I was able to drop a 30 on his head.[2]

On one play during a game on March 1, 2003, Jordan tried to steal the ball from Rose and hit him in the neck and head. He was called for a personal foul, but the Bulls felt it was a flagrant, and Rose got ejected for arguing the point.

I know for a fact he should have gotten a flagrant foul, because it was so blatant. He hit me in the head and knocked my tooth out. But he was talking to the referees the whole game. At that point in his career, he was looking for help from them even more than he did when he was with the Bulls. The damage was done. He didn't get a flagrant foul. He was Michael Jordan.

---

[1] During Jordan's last season, he played in all 82 games, starting in 67. His teammate and longtime friend, Charles Oakley, was also born in 1963. Oakley played in 42 games that season, starting in only one.

[2] The game Rose is likely talking about took place on January 2, 2003, in which he scored 26 points in a 107–82 loss. Jordan scored 10.

Hall of Fame guard Reggie Miller also remembers those epic battles between the Bulls and Pacers.

Looking back over all of my years in the NBA, you would have thought we would have played each other more than once in the playoffs. That was an epic series.

I knew I had to bring it every time I played him. He might have been the one player I did not want to talk to, because he was the one player who could really embarrass you if he wanted. He was one of the smartest basketball players I have ever seen, and he knew what your weaknesses were and he always tried to exploit them.

Jim Boylen

Longtime assistant coach Jim Boylen has been part of three championship coaching staffs, including the 2014 Spurs. But he also won two rings with the Rockets in 1994 and 1995—the years that Jordan was retired and made his comeback.

WHAT'S FUNNY IS that [Rockets head coach] Rudy [Tomjanovich] always looked at Michael Jordan and that Bulls team defensively first. Before we worried about their scoring, it was a matter of just being as worried about them defensively. We knew they were going to score, and if Michael was going to have 50 points or whatever, if he was on a roll and not missing, then, okay, we were not going to win. But we thought they were so good defensively, and they had a great ability to pressure the ball and impact the game at the defensive end, with the way they played the passing lanes and really, just the mental aspect they brought to it.

That was overlooked, I think. Michael was smart, very smart defensively. He could read passes, he could steal the ball and go right into transition, and they would create points off that. They maybe did not have great big guys, but they always seemed to do a good job with Dream [Hakeem Olajuwon], so we were concerned with how they were going to match up with him, how they would send help, not turning the ball over against them, not setting them up going the other way.

We had guys who—you have to say this humbly—but guys who at least could stay with Jordan. Vernon Maxwell, Mario Elie, and those guys. They would try and were strong, athletic, and very good wing defenders. I would not say they shut him down by any means, but we felt like we could hang in there with him if we made him play over us and made him work for every basket. So for us, it was always about scoring against them, attacking their defense, their pressure. We would go into the coaches' meetings, and we would not necessarily talk about guarding Michael Jordan or anything. We would talk about scoring against them on offense and keeping him from creating turnovers.

We were always approaching it like, "How do we make the ball come out of the net?" so that they're not getting out in transition, so that they're not running out, those kinds of things. Slowing down a great scorer; sometimes the best way is to score yourself. It is a different side of it, and people might not remember that as being a reason those teams were so great. But if you were in the coaches' meetings at the time, you were going to hear a lot about their defense, first and foremost. Michael Jordan was a great offensive player, but he was one of the best perimeter defenders, too.

They had Pippen, they had Rodman, they had Ron Harper—all of that plus Michael. At times, they had three or four of the top ten or fifteen defensive players in the league at the same time. That's a handful. You had to have a game plan for that.

I get asked a lot if we would have liked to have seen them in the two years Michael was retired, the two years we won the championship.[3] I don't know how to answer that question, because I don't know if, "like," is the right word. Would we have liked to have seen Michael Jordan in the Finals? People have said, "The Bulls weren't there" for

---

[3] Houston won titles in 1994 and '95, years Jordan spent retired and pursuing his baseball career.

our two championship seasons, as though that means our accomplishments are lessened by that, and I think that is unfair. You still have to go through the process, you still have to get to the next round and keep winning. We were the No. 6 seed in '95, and we won at Utah, at Phoenix, and at San Antonio; not once having home-court advantage. Come on, man, the West was tough back then. It's unfair to diminish what we accomplished.

If you ask people in our camp, from [general manager] Carroll Dawson to Rudy T. on down, nobody is saying, "We caught a break because the Bulls were not there." We were not thinking about the Bulls, we were thinking about getting through the West—hey, the Bulls did not make it through the East. Jordan wasn't playing? Okay, that's not our fault. We were not worried about that. Nobody cried for us when Charles Barkley got hurt in 1997, we wound up losing the series against Utah in the conference finals. Or else, yeah, we would have seen the Bulls in the Finals that year.

It would have been a great challenge, it would have been fun. Michael Jordan was such a gifted offensive player. But if we had seen them in the Finals, I can tell you this: we would have been focused on dealing with their defense. That was as big a challenge with those great Bulls teams as anything.

John Hammond

Hammond is a longtime respected NBA executive who got his start working in scouting with the expansion Timberwolves in 1989 and was an assistant coach in the 1990s to the likes of Larry Brown with the Clippers and Doug Collins with the Pistons.

COACHING AGAINST HIM, if you go back to the early '90s, I think it started out in his career, you said, "Give him space, make him beat you with jump shots." I was in Minnesota and then the Clippers in those years, and that was more or less the game plan when you were going against the Bulls. I think most teams in the league, everybody felt that. Obviously, you could play that way and he still had the ability to go by you and beat you anyway, get to the basket, finish at the basket, and get to the free-throw line. But if there was one thing you could take a little solace in, it was that you could give him space and force him to make the jump shot. As soon as he started making the jump shot? Basically, party over.

He became unguardable. As soon as he became someone who you had to go out and guard the shot, you felt like you had to really go out and pressure him. Then, of course, it opened up everything else for him. That's how he became the greatest to ever play the game. He was great before that, but you felt like you had some ways to at least approach him. But when he got to a point where he could do everything out on the floor, that is when he became the greatest to ever play the game.

The way he seemed to approach games was, he almost made it a point to spread the ball around early and see if he could get other people involved in the game—his big men, the shooters that they had. Because he knew that he had the ability to do it himself, he had the ability to score any time he wanted to or needed to. But the most important thing was to get other people involved. A lot of times, as coaches, he would put you in a position defensively where you could not double-team him, because he was happily making plays for other people. Then once you got down to crunch time, when the game was on the line, that was when he made the plays. You could double him, but you had not been doing that all game and your defense might not be ready for it. That's why you saw a lot of defenses, in those NBA Finals, they would double him late in the game and he made heroes out of those jump shooters around him.

It was so difficult preparing for Michael. I remember, in the earlier days, we were doing game films deck-to-deck on VHS. Now, you get those all online or you can burn DVDs and all of that. But back then, you would sit in front of a TV monitor with two remotes—one in each hand—and on one TV you would be hitting play and on the other you were hitting record. That's how you would make your game film. It was as boring as it sounds, it would be two o'clock in the morning and you were trying to prep for the next game, you could barely stay awake. My memory was, any time we were getting ready to play the Bulls, I was glued to the TV. Because even making game films, I wanted to be alert so I could see that one move that only he could do. If you watched the film long enough, every game, he would have at least one of those plays that would make you say, "No one else could do that."

Dennis Scott

Forward/Guard

Career: 1991–2000

Michael Jordan vs. Dennis Scott										
Regular Season	Games	Wins	Losses	Win %	Field Goal %	PPG	Points (High)	RPG	APG	SPG
Jordan	13	11	2	84.6	46.4	28.2	44 (4/2/91)	5.5	5.4	2.7
Scott	13	2	11	15.4	40.8	12.8	24 (12/13/95)	3.2	1.6	1.2

Playoffs	Games	Wins	Losses	Win %	Field Goal %	PPG	Points (High)	RPG	APG	SPG
Jordan	10	6	4	60.0	49.1	30.4	45 (5/27/96)	6.1	4.1	2.4
Scott	10	4	6	40.0	35.1	11.8	22 (5/16/95)	2.8	1.8	1.0

Scott was one of the best shooters of his generation and made 39.7 percent of his 3-pointers in 10 seasons. His best years came in Orlando, where he teamed with Shaquille O'Neal to lead Orlando to the Finals in 1995 and to the Eastern Conference Finals in 1996—where they were swept by Chicago.

THE YEAR WE beat them was 1995, and we were a very good, young team. We were the No. 1 seed and had Shaq [O'Neal], Penny [Hardaway], myself, and had gotten Horace Grant that summer. We had some talent; we were a good team.

It was a fun series because you saw the intensity with him; you saw it in his eyes. He had been playing baseball, so it was obvious he was not

100 percent in terms of that supreme confidence.[4] He had some great games [that series]; some games where he had 39 points, 40 points, so he could still get his points. The intensity was there, but not the confidence . . . not yet. You could still see the competitor. But a lot of the things that really defined him—like the conditioning and the mental toughness and the defense—that was not there at that point. And really, the Bulls just had a hard time dealing with Shaq.

We won against them [in the Eastern Conference Semifinals], won the next round [against the Indiana Pacers in the Eastern Conference Finals], and wound up going to the Finals. But that series, we were facing No. 45—after he did the comeback, he wore 45 for that year.[5] What was funny is, here was a young team like us, you could tell he was looking at us like, "I am not ready to give up my championships to these young bucks." It was the old cliché, he was a sleeping giant. Losing to us, that just woke up that sleeping giant, and we did not know it at the time, but that series changed things.

He wasn't ready to let anyone else have the stage. That's basically what he did; he took it back. He hooked up with Tim Grover again in the off-season, got himself back into the kind of shape he is used to, changed his game a little, and [the Bulls] were unstoppable the next year.[6] He was more of a post player, but he was still as tough as ever, maybe even better. He was No. 45 in 1995. He was back to being No. 23 in 1996, and that was the big difference.

That year, we got them in the Eastern Conference Finals. That was the year they won 72 games, but we were good, too, better than the

---

[4] The 1994–95 season was Jordan's first since returning from a one-year hiatus when he played baseball for the Birmingham Barons, the AA affiliate of the Chicago White Sox.

[5] Jordan wore 45 for the regular season and for Game 1 of the Eastern Conference Semifinals. He switched back to his old 23 for Game 2, but was fined $25,000 by the league for changing numbers.

[6] The 1995–96 Bulls would go 72–10 for the season, setting the record for most wins by a team in league history.

previous year, we had won 60 games.[7] But it was just different. It wasn't just Michael, that whole team was great. They won that first game of the series by 40 and that set the tone.[8] They swept us and went on to win three more championships. Once Michael was No. 23 again, he won three more. That tells you what you need to know about Michael—he was that kind of competitor.

What set a player like him apart is supreme confidence. It is very similar to what you see from LeBron James. Every great player I have been around, they have that confidence in themselves. When you played against Michael Jordan, you knew you had to bring your A+ game every night because he was not going to let up on you at all. If you did not have "Bulls" on the front of your jersey, he wanted to reach into your chest and pull your heart out. He wanted to annihilate you, every night. That's why he was the greatest.

---

[7] The 1994–95 Magic had a record of 57–25 and improved that record to 60–22 the following season.
[8] The Bulls won Game 1, 121–83.

Dwane Casey

After a successful career at Kentucky, Casey was an assistant coach with the Wildcats throughout the 1980s, eventually moving to the NBA, where he joined George Karl's staff in Seattle in 1994. The following year, the Sonics earned a spot in the NBA Finals, facing Jordan in his first trip back to the championship round after returning from retirement.

I REMEMBER WHEN HE was coming out of high school. He wasn't highly recruited and, if he had not gone to North Carolina to play for Dean Smith, as I recall it, the next place for him to go play was going to be with Hugh Durham in Georgia. They had a good team,

too. There was a lot of hubbub about him, but it was not really a recruiting war or anything. I think most everyone thought he would be a good player, but you know, just a pretty good player.

When he got to North Carolina, it was obvious he was a great athlete, a guy who had a competitive streak about him even when he was at that age. That is something we all got to witness by the time he got to the NBA, of course. In college, it just came in little glimpses, because he was playing for Dean Smith and he was playing within the system and they were winning.

But because of that, there was no way of knowing what he was destined for at that age. I don't think anybody knew that Michael Jordan would turn out to be one of the all-time greatest players in the league. You knew he was a talented individual and had a gift for competing, but I don't think anyone would have predicted his greatness when it comes to where he stands all-time in the NBA. And you have to put him up there as one of the greatest— if not the greatest—athlete to play the game.

That was something we got to see in the NBA Finals when I was an assistant in Seattle, in 1996. That was the year the Bulls went 72–10, and just looked like such a great team. But we were good, too—we won 64 games that year—and we had a deep and very talented team. We had gone through some tough playoffs when we lost in the first round the two years before that, and we had a tough series against Utah in the Western Conference Finals. But we felt ready for the Bulls. We split our two regular season games against them, winning the first meeting in Seattle early on in the year. We were actually able to hold Michael down a little bit, he did not have a great game and we won that one by five.[9] The second meeting, at the United Center, they won that one pretty easily and Michael Jordan was a lot better that time.[10] We felt like we were pretty even with them.

Preparing for Michael in that series in 1996 reminds me a lot now of preparing for LeBron James when I was an assistant coach in Dallas and we played the Heat in the Finals in 2011. Players like that, you have to prepare for what you want to live with. Because they're so good that you're not going to take away everything. They're going to find a way to get something from you, you just have to decide what and how much. You can double-team them, send help over to them, all of that. But they are going to find a way to make you pay, either by scoring or passing. Or both.

In 1996, Jordan at that time, it was after he had come back from his retirement and made adjustments to his game. He was getting

---

[9] Jordan scored 22 points on 6-for-19 shooting.
[10] The Bulls won, 113–87, with Jordan scoring 35 points with 14 rebounds.

into his thirties, he was not playing above the rim anymore. But that did not make it easier. He had become more of a post-up guy—which was just as bad—he was just as a dangerous. Maybe more dangerous, because he was still athletic but was strong and really smart.

So, the thing we, as coaches, our focus on heading into the Finals that year was: how do we stop him in the post? We had a bad break because the guy who probably would have done the best job on him individually was Nate McMillan, who was a very good defender and big enough to handle Jordan in the post. Nate was about 6-6, he was strong and could match Michael in a lot of ways. But Nate was not healthy, he had a bad back problem at that time—he had nerve problems—and though he was out there trying to play, he was not 100 percent. He played Game 1, but only a few minutes. He did not play at all in Game 2 or Game 3, and we lost those. He came back for Game 4, though, and we won that, and Game 5, too. But it was tough because you can't tell a guy, "Hey, go guard Michael Jordan," if he is not healthy.

We had Detlef Schrempf, he was 6-9 and could guard in the post, but he was too slow to keep up with Jordan. We had Gary Payton, who is an all-time great defensive player, but he was too small (6-4, 180) to handle guarding Jordan down there. Gary was probably the best perimeter defender in the league, but Jordan was not playing on the perimeter all that much at the time. David Wingate was on our team at that time, we tried him, Hersey Hawkins, we tried. We tried a little bit of everyone on him.

That was all George [Karl] could do. He was reaching and stretching and grabbing for anything he could find that would work with Nate out. You have to give Michael different looks, which was the adjustment we could make. But it's not an easy thing to do. If you are making too many adjustments on a guy at the defensive end, it can hurt your offense.

We tried double-teaming him, but he is such a good passer that he can just pick you apart with his passing when you send someone over to double team. You have to make your choice—you double-team him and get the ball out of his hands, but he is going to make the right pass. Don't forget, on that team, you had Steve Kerr spotted up out there, you had Kukoc on that team. Harper knocking down shots. The triangle offense at the time was so difficult to double-team, because they would overload the corner, which made it tough to spead out and double-team. You had to have a designated double-team guy. That is what we tried to do.

Or if you decided not to double-team, you can leave him one-on-one and say, "Okay, Michael, you can score 30 or 40 points tonight and we will try to shut everyone else down." Then you're giving him layups. That's really not much better.

We went into that series, and we were probably not ready. We felt we could win—as a competitor, you always feel like you can win when you go into a series. But we went into the series and they jumped on us, we got spanked the first couple games. Game 1, they really pulled away from us in the fourth quarter. We tried to come out with Detlef on Michael, as far as guarding him initially is concerned. But we also put Payton on him some. We realized we needed to change things up.

Game 2, they kind of took control in the first half and just kept control. Game 3 was back in our building and it was a 2–3–2 setup, where they play two in Chicago, then three in Seattle. We lost Game 3, by a lot, and that really was damaging for us.

But once we got over the initial shock, we got our sea legs back and we battled them pretty good. We won Game 4 and Game 5, and Game 6 was an ugly one, but we had a chance in that one. We felt like, the longer we could keep playing, the more of a chance we had to pull it off. It just wasn't enough, though.

Looking back, it would have been nice to have another chance at that. We felt like we had a legit chance to win that series. But it really makes you realize just how great Jordan was, how great he was as a player, how difficult it was to stop him. You know, as coaches, you are up all night trying to put together different game plans, and you think you have everything covered. But then he goes out and does what he wants anyway, scores the ball, gets his teammates involved. And you have to think, *there goes the game plan.*

They just were a great team, obviously. But there is no question, Michael Jordan was the main difference in that series. He was still good enough physically that he could beat you that way, but he had been around long enough—he was mature and smart—that he could beat you with his head, too. It was just so difficult to figure out how to stop him in that phase of his career.

Lamond Murray

Forward

Career: **1995–2006**

Michael Jordan vs. Lamond Murray										
Regular Season	Games	Wins	Losses	Win %	Field Goal %	PPG	Points (High)	RPG	APG	SPG
Jordan	6	5	1	83.3	47.3	30.8	49 (11/21/97)	6.7	4.8	2.0
Murray	6	1	5	16.7	35.0	10.8	24 (11/21/97)	5.5	2.5	1.8

Ask Lamond Murray for a memory that stands out from his 12-year NBA career, and he quickly answers: The game on November 11, 1997, in which his young Clippers team nearly knocked off the powerhouse Bulls in Los Angeles. What thwarted the upset? Michael Jordan's 49 points.

WE WERE AT the Sports Arena in Los Angeles. That was after their 72-win season, after they had won two straight championships. Honestly, we should have beaten them. We had the game won at that time, which was a big deal for us. We were the Clippers, they were the Bulls. We were not supposed to win that game, but we had them down; we actually played very well that game. But they had Michael Jordan. I remember, Jordan wound up with [49 points], but he had to score 40 points in the second half and in overtime of that game [to win].

Still, we were at a point at the end of the game—in overtime—where all we had to do was inbound the ball and we would have won.

I remember I had a good game, I was in the fourth year of my career, so I was starting to establish myself. But I had a good game.[11] What I remember most was, this was the Bulls at their height, with Michael and Scottie Pippen and Dennis Rodman. Everywhere they went, they had people following them; they were just an exciting team, and everyone was watching the Bulls at that time. Michael had been gone playing baseball, but he came back and, for a few years after that, they just had everything working.

Inside the arena, it was jammed. It was standing-room-only inside. It was past capacity, it was hot in there—it was a great atmosphere, but it was so hot in there, you couldn't breathe, you couldn't help but sweat every step you took, you couldn't think. There were a lot of people in there rooting for the Bulls, but that kind of pushed us on some more. And there we were in the fourth quarter, beating the Chicago Bulls. We had lost a bunch of games to start the year.[12] We had myself, we had Brent Barry, we had Lorenzen Wright—you know, we were young, and they had Michael Jordan.

We actually did a good job on him in the first half. We were up by something like 20 points in the first half.[13] We held Michael to seven, eight points in the first half and that was pretty good for us. He was just missing some shots in some cases. But there was some good defense, too. We did a good job—in the first half at least. In the second half, all the shots he was missing started going in. He really took over, and they started coming back.

We were there with a lead in overtime, we had been winning most of the game, and all we had to do was inbound the basketball from the

---

[11] Murray had 24 points and nine rebounds, on 8-for-16 shooting.
[12] The Clippers were 1–10 at that point in the season and would finish with a 17–65 record, which was the third worst in the league.
[13] The Clippers lead by 18 at the end of the half.

sideline. I remember it clearly, we were up by two points, we called a timeout with about twenty seconds left, and all we had to do was get it in, they would have to foul us, and we would make our free throws and win the game. That was it. But they had changed the rule, and at the time, coming out of a timeout, you could not throw the ball into the backcourt to get it in.

We didn't know that rule, I guess, coming out of the timeout. No one said anything to me; it was not what we drew up. Now, looking back, it was so hot in there that you could not think. Maybe that was our excuse for not remembering the rule. Whatever it was, we were trying to enter the ball, and sure enough, we throw it into the backcourt. Violation. Turnover. And I was thinking, I mean everybody was thinking, *You got the game won, you can't give Michael Jordan a chance to take it from you.*

They get the ball, give it to Michael, he comes across the middle and gets fouled. He actually missed both of the free throws, though, but he somehow gets the rebound, pulls it out, cuts into the middle of the floor, and gets to the basket. He made the layup and sent it into double overtime. We didn't score a point in double overtime. They controlled it from there. It is one thing; we played so hard and so well to get a chance to win. But you're playing the Bulls in double overtime? Double overtime didn't go very well for us, let's say that. Like I said, I don't think we even scored a point.

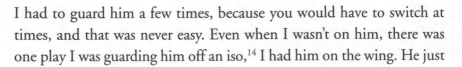

I had to guard him a few times, because you would have to switch at times, and that was never easy. Even when I wasn't on him, there was one play I was guarding him off an iso,[14] I had him on the wing. He just

---

[14] An isolation play, in which one player gets the ball and his teammates move away, leaving him one-on-one with his defender.

faced up, looked at me, blew by me, and dunked. I thought I was in good position, defensively. He was just so athletic.

With him, sometimes, it did not matter if you were in good position, you know? He was going to find a way to get by you and go to the rim. They would always say: "You have to make him go left." But what he would do is, he would take two dribbles or so to the left, then he would cut back to his right and you'd be off-balance. Or even worse, you would be trying to force him to his left by cutting off the angle to his right, and he would look at you and just say, "I'm still going right." And he would just go right, he would go around you—he was that quick, that strong. He stayed low when he was attacking, he was able to get low and keep his dribble, and that made him tough to cover.

It was a team thing, trying to guard Michael Jordan. With the Clippers, we just didn't figure it out; we didn't have much of a team concept at the time. We were winning the game, so something was working. But in crunch time, they had such an advantage. Michael scored 49 points. So, we were the Clippers and they had maybe the greatest player ever. That tells you how the night wound up going.

Dennis Rodman

Forward

Career: 1987–2000
Career Highlights: ....two-time All-Star, two-time Defensive
Player of the Year, five-time NBA Finals
Champion, Inducted to the Naismith
Memorial Basketball Hall of Fame (2011)
Jordan Highlights: ....Won three NBA Finals with
Jordan (1996–98)

Michael Jordan vs. Dennis Rodman										
Regular Season	Games	Wins	Losses	Win %	Field Goal %	PPG	Points (High)	RPG	APG	SPG
Jordan	37	16	21	43.2	47.8	31.8	61 (3/4/87)	6.1	5.7	2.2
Rodman	37	21	16	56.8	55.8	9.7	25 (11/21/87)	10.0	1.3	0.6

Playoffs	Games	Wins	Losses	Win %	Field Goal %	PPG	Points (High)	RPG	APG	SPG
Jordan	22	10	12	45.5	48.1	30.0	47 (5/26/90)	6.7	6.1	2.1
Rodman	22	12	10	54.5	48.5	7.1	20 (5/28/90)	9.5	0.6	0.6

By the mid-'90s, it seemed that there were no teams left in the NBA for which the league's quirkiest character—Dennis Rodman—could play. But it turned out, there was one: Chicago. In three seasons with Jordan and the Bulls, Rodman led the league in rebounding and forever altered his legacy, earning a spot in the Hall of Fame.

THAT FIRST YEAR I came in,[15] there was just no doubt really that we were going to be a great team, one of the best ever. We were rock stars. We were a rock

---

[15] Rodman joined the Bulls in 1996.

star team. They were calling us the Beatles. Everybody wanted to come and see us, there was always electricity in every city we went to.

They [the Bulls] were already a pretty good team, but Michael had not really been himself the year before, and he came back and was 100 percent and it was like everything just clicked. I don't know what they were thinking about me when I first came in, because I had been with the Pistons. I was the enemy before, you know? But we all got along great. We knew we could win every night out there. Didn't matter if we were losing by 10 or 20, we knew we would have a chance to come back and win. A lot of that came from Michael, but you had Scottie there, too, and Phil.

What was great about going there and playing with them was that they really didn't care what I did away from the court. I could just live my life. Whatever I did, they were not interested. It was just like, as long as I was producing. And they knew there wasn't anybody out there who would be playing harder than me. So I would go and I would do my thing and we would talk on the court and talk about the game, but after the game, it was, okay, you go your way, I am going mine. I liked that. They liked it, too.

Michael and me and Scottie were not close or anything at the time. We really didn't talk, hardly at all. Just basketball. We talked basketball. They just wanted someone who put basketball first and cared about winning. That was what I did. I worked, worked, worked, worked. I played every game like it was my last. And Michael liked that, because he was someone who worked, too. He understood me in that way. He was not very big when I was in Detroit, but later, he was really, really strong, especially for his position.

He was a professional; he just knew everything he needed to know out there. He knew how to take you apart if you were trying to defend him. He knew how to get his shot when it was crunch time. He knew who he could rely on when we needed a big play. He was an innovate you know? A creator. He played the game different than anyone For me, that is what I always tried to do. I was a much different than him, obviously, but I wanted to be someone who always things. We were similar in that way.

Mark Jackson

Guard

NBA: Career: 1988–2004
Head Coaching Career: 2012–14
Career Highlights: .... 1988 Rookie of the Year, 1989 All-Star

Michael Jordan vs. Mark Jackson										
Regular Season	Games	Wins	Losses	Win %	Field Goal %	PPG	Points (High)	RPG	APG	SPG
Jordan	42	31	11	73.8	47.3	29.6	49 (3/30/90)	6.0	4.7	2.5
Jackson	42	11	31	26.2	49.7	10.6	33 (3/7/88)	4.0	8.4	1.2

In 17 seasons, Jackson established himself as one of the greatest players of all-time. The one thing missing? Like so many other players of that era, a championship ring. Jackson played on some outstanding teams in New York and Indiana, but was never able to get past Jordan's Bulls.

FOR ME, WATCHING Jordan's Bulls—and obviously the Celtics with Larry Bird and Kevin McHale and Robert Parish, and those guys . . . Dennis Johnson; watching Danny Ainge and the great Showtime Lakers—those were incredible teams. Because not only were they great in their own right, but they all had to play each other in order to move on, so you got some really great matchups and a hard road to go through in order to get to the next round of the playoffs.

Michael Jordan will always be the best I've ever faced, and he's the best

I've ever seen. Flat out. There were times when I can recall he single-handedly beat us with the Knicks when other guys were not ready at that particular time. He propelled them to be great and propelled them to a championship level. He was an absolutely incredible, fierce competitor. For his teammates, he invited a winning spirit and did everything on the floor to attempt to tear the heart out and put daggers into his opposition. And you can see the impact that he's had not just in that time, but even in watching players after him, how they attempted to duplicate or put some of the things in their game that he had mastered.

But those were great Bulls teams. Like I said, there are times when he singlehandedly put them in position to win it all.

I felt like no matter where I went, I was running into Michael Jordan. When I was with the Knicks in the early part of my career, playing with Patrick Ewing, it was the Celtics, and then the Pistons, and then finally the Bulls were the tough team to get past. Then with Indiana, it was the same thing.

I thought we were right there with them in 1998, in the playoffs, in the Eastern Conference Finals. We were with them, step-for-step. We were physical, we were not afraid to foul—and to foul them hard. Larry Bird was our coach, and he would tell us not to be afraid, to put those guys on their rear ends if they wanted to come into the paint against us. We got under their skin a little bit.

But they were such a great team, they got past us in seven games. We thought we had the ability to win a championship that year, and we were close. But Michael Jordan and those Bulls, they frustrated a lot of teams that were probably good enough to win NBA championships in the '90s.

Fred Hoiberg

Guard

Career: **1996–2005**

Michael Jordan vs. Fred Hoiberg										
Regular Season	Games	Wins	Losses	Win %	Field Goal %	PPG	Points (High)	RPG	APG	SPG
Jordan	13	10	3	76.9	42.5	23.5	38 (3/7/97)	5.9	4.4	1.7
Hoiberg	13	3	10	23.1	35.0	2.4	7 (3/1/03)	1.6	1.0	0.2
Playoffs	Games	Wins	Losses	Win %	Field Goal %	PPG	Points (High)	RPG	APG	SPG
Jordan	1	1	0	100	60.0	29.0	29 (5/27/98)	7.0	4.0	1.0
Hoiberg	1	0	1	0.0	28.6	6.0	6 (5/27/98)	3.0	1.0	1.0

Hoiberg, now the head coach at Iowa State, was a third-year player for the Pacers when they went to the Eastern Conference Finals against Jordan and the Bulls in 1998. He would go on to play 10 seasons for three teams in his career.

IWAS IN MY third year (in 1997–98) with Indiana, and we had a really good team. There were a lot of veterans, but guys who were still very good, like Reggie Miller, Mark Jackson, Rik Smits, that core group of guys. I remember all throughout that year, Larry Bird (in his first season as coach) talked about how important it was to get home-court advantage. He told us every game meant something, and after the first three or four months, we were ahead of them. But at the end of the year, they went on this long winning streak and really finished up the second half of the year with a strong run.[16]

So they wound up with that No. 1 seed. And Larry was right; it did wind up meaning something because of the way that series wound up going. It started out, they won the first two games on their home floor, and we were able to come back and win two on our home floor. And both teams held serve on their home floor throughout that series.

Then in that Game 7, we were at the United Center, and we had them down, we had a double-digit lead in that game and it looked like we would finally get past them. Jordan was not having a great game, nor was Pippen.[17]

But despite that, what Michael did down the stretch; it was just one of the greatest performances I have ever seen. He just absolutely took the game over. It was the kind of thing you had seen before from him in other series in the past, but being there to watch it was different. There was no stopping him, not only scoring for himself, but he made a couple of kick-outs and Steve Kerr hit a couple big shots.

His defense, too . . . he was really focused and made some big, big plays. Ron Harper had started on Reggie Miller, but Reggie was having a big game, so Michael took him down the stretch at the end of the game. He took that challenge and made the plays when they mattered most. He really shut Reggie down in the second half of that game.[18]

He did whatever it took to win, that was what stood out. That is what made him the best player in the game.

---

[16] The Bulls were 28–5 to finish the regular season, including a 13-game winning str◆

[17] The two combined for 45 points, but shot just 15-for-43 from the floor.

[18] Miller finished with 22 points, but was held scoreless in the final 15:30.

Howard Eisley

Guard

Career: **1995–2006**

Michael Jordan vs. Howard Eisley										
Regular Season	Games	Wins	Losses	Win %	Field Goal %	PPG	Points (High)	RPG	APG	SPG
Jordan	10	5	5	50.0	46.9	29.1	44 (11/23/96)	7.4	3.8	1.9
Eisley	10	5	5	50.0	42.3	5.4	14 (1/25/98)	0.8	3.0	0.3
Playoffs	Games	Wins	Losses	Win %	Field Goal %	PPG	Points (High)	RPG	APG	SPG
Jordan	12	8	4	66.7	44.1	32.9	45 (6/14/98)	5.5	4.2	1.5
Eisley	12	4	8	33.3	42.6	5.0	9 (6/1/97)	1.3	3.2	0.3

Eisley was a reserve guard for the Jazz in 1997 and '98, playing behind John Stockton for the two teams that probably had the best chance of any teams to knock off Jordan's Bulls in the Finals. But two tries resulted in two heartbreaks, the second coming on Jordan's famous foul-line jumper over Bryon Russell in Utah in Game 6.

FOR ME, THE Utah teams that went to the Finals (in 1997 and 1998) were the best teams I ever played on. I was a young player, and to be around a group like that was big for me. There was a lot of talent there, but there was also a lot of depth, we were a well-rounded team. Of course, we were led by Karl Malone and John Stockton, those were our star players. But we had guys on that team who were very talented and just wanted to do what they could to fill their role, like Jeff Hornacek—who was obviously a great shooter and could do a little bit of everything—but also Bryon Russell, Shandon Anderson, guys like that, too. That was a big key to our success.

We had a very family-type atmosphere, and we had played together for so long—John, Karl, Jerry Sloan, they had been together for a long time, and a lot of us came along during that time. Coach Sloan had his system and we all knew it, and we had that continuity, which was very big for us. The West was very difficult. It was very challenging, with teams like Houston and the Lakers, San Antonio. Going through the playoffs year after year brings you together. That helped us. But Coach Sloan always did a good job of teaching us the game and showing us how he wanted to play, and John and Karl set the example for us. They made it easy to follow.

But, two years in a row, we run into the Bulls and Michael Jordan. He was obviously the best player of his era, but probably the best player of all-time, too. We were both great defensive teams, and if you look at the scores, they were very close but very low.[19] I think the unfortunate thing for us is, in both series, we got down early—we lost the first two games at their place in '97—and in '98 we won the first game but lost the next three. It's hard in a seven-game series to dig a hole [like that] and come out of it.

Of course, you have to show Michael Jordan extra attention when you're playing defense against him. But we were a very good defensive team, like I said, and we really tried to stick to our principles and not stray away from our identity on defense. But again, it *is* Michael Jordan and everybody knows how successful he was. We had to make adjustments against him like everybody else, but we really tried to stay within our system and play our style of defense. He was going to score and it would be tough to prevent that, but you always wanted to make it as difficult for him as possible.

---

[19] In the 1997 Finals, the Bulls outscored Utah by an average of 87.8 to 87.3. In the '98 Finals, it was 88.0 for Chicago to 80.2 for Utah.

The game that still sticks out in my mind is Game 6, of course, that is the one that everyone remembers and talks about. We were down 3–1 in that series but came back to win Game 5 on their home floor. We were able to hold Michael and Scottie Pippen down a little bit in that one.[20] If we can win Game 6, then we would wind up with Game 7 on our home floor.

Everybody knows what happened at the end of the game, but even before that, we had some plays that didn't go our way. I had a 3-pointer I made but they called it after the 24-second buzzer, and the replay showed it wasn't; it should have been good. That one bothers me, and they gave Ron Harper a bucket when it did come after the 24-second clock, the replays showed that, too. So that was a five-point swing for them in a close game. And we had the opportunity to win it in that last possession; we had the ball with thirty or so seconds to go. But we had a turnover on our end off a double-team, Michael made the steal, and he came down and made a great shot against Bryon Russell. Things happen.

People still ask me now whether it was a push-off on Michael Jordan on that last shot. It was . . . a little.

Whether a veteran or a rookie, Jordan had a huge impression on everyone he faced.

John Starks

I was mentally prepared to play against him the first time we played, because when I was in college and I couldn't watch their games, I would have my wife tape them so I could watch them when I came home. I used to study him all the time. When I had the opportunity to play against him, I had already played against him many times in my mind.

---

[20] Jordan and Pippen combined to score 34 points in Game 5, on 11-for-42 shooting, and were 0-for-9 on 3-pointers.

I played a pretty good game that first game. He said before the game that I would be calling him "Mr. Jordan" by the end of the night, and I guess he said that to all the rookies. But after that game I went up to him and said, "You didn't get Mr. Jordan out of me tonight." It was a great experience going up against him that first time.

Lindsey Hunter

I remember the night he put 55 points against us after we beat him in Detroit, and the scoreboard at the Chicago Stadium was just blinking as his numbers went up. I knew he was going to do that against us that night. I had the pleasure of beating him all those years before they got past us, so I have that on him. I was always cool with Michael, I played pickup ball with him all the time.

Jon Barry

I don't know which of the eleven teams I played on I was on at the time, but I remember telling the team photographer, "Get as many shots as you can with me and him in the shot." I have them in my office now. I think he scored his 10,000th point in Chicago Stadium in 1993 or 1994 against the team I was on, and I had never heard anything that crazy in all my years. When you would hear the pregame introductions, and it was his turn to be announced, you just heard, "Six-six, from North Carolina," and that is all you heard. You could not hear them say his name. I have never heard an ovation like that.

It was great to play against him. You had nothing to lose. He was the greatest player ever to play the game, so I thought *What the hell, I'll give it a shot. If he busts my ass, he is supposed to, and if he doesn't, then hey, I stopped him two out of seven times, I am happy.*

He was never demeaning in his talk to me. He was a lot like Larry Bird in the way he talked smack. He would say, "What are you doing down here, JB? I'm going to post you up." Then he would call for the ball in the post, and he would score, and we would go down to the other end of the court.

David Wesley

Guard

Career: **1994–2007**

Michael Jordan vs. David Wesley										
Regular Season	Games	Wins	Losses	Win %	Field Goal %	PPG	Points (High)	RPG	APG	SPG
Jordan	16	12	4	75.0	50.4	28.9	51 (12/29/01)	4.9	4.8	1.9
Wesley	16	4	12	25.0	42.6	15.1	31 (4/1/97)	3.4	4.8	2.0

Playoffs	Games	Wins	Losses	Win %	Field Goal %	PPG	Points (High)	RPG	APG	SPG
Jordan	5	4	1	80.0	46.5	29.6	35 (5/3/98)	5.6	4.6	1.0
Wesley	5	1	4	20.0	43.9	8.4	16 (5/13/98)	1.2	5.4	0.2

Wesley is one of the best undrafted players in NBA history, logging 14 seasons, a 12.3-point scoring average, and a reputation as an outstanding defender— even when he had to check Jordan in the 1998 Eastern Conference Semifinals.

PROBABLY ONE OF the most remarkable things I saw a player do was what Michael did during his comeback, when I was in Charlotte. It was 2001, and he was in Washington at that time, in his late thirties. Just before they were supposed to play us, he had the worst game of his career. They were playing [the Pacers], and he didn't even hit double figures, it was like the first time in years that happened.[21] We were next on the schedule, going into Washington, and you had to know he was going to be

---

[21] Jordan's double-figures streak had been 866 games.

mad coming off a game like that. You didn't want to be next on the schedule with a player like him.

He went out and scored 51 against us. I remember that game—I didn't play, as I was hurt. Lee Nailon guarded him most of that game, and Lee, unfortunately, got a lot of that 51 from Michael. He was young in his second year out of TCU and had not been playing a whole lot. But here he is; gets put into the starting lineup and has to guard Michael Jordan. Even though he was thirty-eight, Michael could still score. And he wasn't happy about that last game.

I remember as the game went on, Coach [Paul] Silas was getting madder and madder at us. Not at Lee, but at everybody else on the team, because no one stepped up and said, "I'll take him." When you're playing against an all-time great and he is scoring on you like that, especially if you've got to use a young player on him, you want someone to step up and try to stop it. But, even at that point, late in his career, he was still capable of putting up 50. Lee did his job, he did the best he could, but Michael is Michael.

He was always a difficult matchup for anyone, though. He is one of those players who, if you put a bigger player on him, he goes around him. If you put a smaller guy on him, he's going to shoot over the top. He played with incredible energy.

I used to enjoy playing against him. Everybody asks me, "Who is the hardest player you had to guard?" They expect me to say Michael Jordan, but that's not really it. Michael wasn't hard for me to guard, because I was six feet tall and trying to guard him at that height, I was giving up a lot of size and talent. I was just out there battling—that was easy, I can go out there and battle with anyone, 100 percent with anyone. When I got stops, they were not expecting me to get stops, so it was like a bonus in the eyes of most people.

But I would make it tough on him where he caught the ball, I would be in his face and just be a pest. He is by far, hands down, the best player I ever played against, arguably the best of all-time. But guarding him was easy because you knew what the strategy was every time.

My foot speed could keep up with his, so I could keep him in front of me. Strength-wise, I could push him off the block a little bit and give time for my teammates to try and double him. I really paid attention to the details. I worked hard, kept him off his spots, and that was what you would hope to do against him. That didn't mean he wasn't going to still score . . . that is what made him Michael Jordan. But at least you could have an idea of what you needed to do against him.

If you could get him to have his back to you in the high post and force him into a turnaround jumper from there, that was what you had to live with. The goal was to always be contesting his shots, as I knew I was not going to block it. The thing is, I tried to be physical, I tried to do my work early and make him try to guess where he'd be, make him try to settle for that turnaround jump shot. He got better as a jump shooter as his career went on, and that's why he continued to have the numbers he did. But that's the shot you want to have him take, and I felt like I could get him to do that. But if that's not working, if he is making that shot, we would have to get a bigger guy on him. That's the mentality I would have—just beat him up as much as possible, bring pressure and try to challenge every look that he gets.

When he was still with the Bulls [in 1998], it was my first year in Charlotte and the last year that their team was together. They were getting older, and there was a chance that maybe, this time, they could be beaten. We got them in the playoffs that year; they were still a team working on a dynasty.

For us, I think everyone goes into a situation like that thinking you've got a chance to win. They were a great team, but we had a pretty good young team and could battle as well as anyone. That is how you think at the time, but you look back on it now and I think you would have to say, "Maybe not," you know, maybe we did not have a legitimate chance in that series. They were a dominant team. It is almost like looking at Miami now; they were that team to beat, the one with the target on their chests at all times.

But they were the team that even when you picked up your own game because you're playing against the champs, they always seemed to find another gear, another way to beat you. That is what I remember about that series—as much as we felt like we had a chance to win, maybe not so much. They were just that good.

In those 1998 playoffs, we played them pretty well in the opener of that series against Chicago. We actually won Game 2 in their building, so we had some momentum coming back to Charlotte for Game 3. But with Michael, he had a little bit of a boost in his step whenever he played us; he was a North Carolina guy, so playing against Charlotte seemed to get him going—if that is even necessary for a guy who was on top of the basketball world at the time. But when he would come to Charlotte—it was his home area—so he liked coming in and showing what he could do.

Sure enough, they won the two games in Charlotte. That fourth game, we were right there with them in the second half but they just pulled away from us. Michael was up over 30 points in that one. They finished the series in five games.

Like I said, as a team, they were just that good—and as a player, he was just that good.

Sam Cassell

Guard

Career: 199–2008
Career Highlights: ....2004 All-Star, three-time NBA Finals
Champion

Michael Jordan vs. Sam Cassell										
Regular Season	Games	Wins	Losses	Win %	Field Goal %	PPG	Points (High)	RPG	APG	SPG
Jordan	16	11	5	68.8	45.6	26.9	38 (1/3/96)	5.5	3.4	1.2
Cassell	16	5	11	31.2	44.9	17.6	31 (1/30/03)	2.9	5.8	1.4

Playoffs	Games	Wins	Losses	Win %	Field Goal %	PPG	Points (High)	RPG	APG	SPG
Jordan	3	3	0	100	52.9	36.3	39 (4/24/98)	5.0	2.7	1.3
Cassell	3	0	3	0.0	33.3	2.0	4 (4/24/98)	1.0	1.7	0.0

Sam Cassell played with nine teams starting in 1993 and finishing his career in 2008. He faced Jordan numerous times, although he played more of his career in the Western Conference than in the East. He is now an assistant coach with the Washington Wizards.

IREMEMBER WE HAD a game in Chicago, and I was being guarded by Randy Brown and Ron Harper and Dennis Rodman, and I had my way with those guys that night. I remember Rodman told Mike, "You better guard Cass or we are going to lose this ball game." I think I had 27 with about six minutes to go in the game, and I thought I had it going, but Jordan had the competitive nature that nobody else has, and he shut me down in those final six.

Me being a competitor, I thought it was fantastic to have the best player in the league coming at me. I took it as an honor that he was on me. I wanted to beat the Bulls more than anything at that particular time. I talked on the court, and he would talk back, but he is better than me, so if we wanted to talk, he won the talking contest. Not to take anything away from LeBron James, but I hear people saying, "LeBron or Michael," and there is no contest. It's Mike.

I was playing for the New Jersey Nets in the playoffs one year—in a best-of-five series—and he had a decent Game 1 in Chicago and the Bulls won, and he had a decent Game 2 and the Bulls won, and as we were walking onto the court in East Rutherford for the start of Game 3, he said to me, "Where are you going tomorrow?" I said, "Practice," and he said, "No, you're not." He blew the game open in the first quarter and just took the series from us.

Section Four: Mental Edge

"He calls us over to the center circle and says, 'I have had a cold for a while, I have not been feeling great. But your buddy over there was talking smack, so now I am about to turn it up on you all.' Then I think he scored 37 in the second half."

—Former Miami Heat forward, Grant Long

PROBABLY NO ASPECT of Jordan's character as an NBA star is more fascinating than the way he was able to focus himself during games. Early in his career, when he was just finding his way in the NBA, he seemed to be constantly focused, driven by the fact that he was still establishing himself against league stars like Magic Johnson and Larry Bird. Beyond that, before he was winning NBA championships, he was able to use the criticisms of media observers and other players to drive him. And when Jordan was focused, particularly in crunch-time situations, there was no one better.

But as he was winning more and more—and as he was aging—it seemed to get more difficult for Jordan to maintain that level of extreme focus. Very often, Jordan would take a piece of banter uttered by a lesser player and use it as motivation to take over and win a game. The collective memory vault of players in that era is stuffed with stories of ill-advised trash-talk aimed at Jordan, talk that almost always led to a healthy serving of embarrassment and, of course, a loss.

In this section, we start with scientific theory explaining why it might be that the game seems slower for a star player who is mentally locked in the way Jordan used to be and move to examples of how Jordan would take the slightest bit of talk and turn it into the kind of fodder that would allow him to get to the mentally locked-in state.

Dr. Stuart Hameroff

Dr. Hameroff is an anesthesiologist and professor at the University of Arizona. He is also a director of the Center for Consciousness Studies and one of the world's foremost authorities on consciousness. He's also a basketball fan who has used Michael Jordan as an example in explaining his theories on how consciousness works.

THE THING ABOUT someone like Michael Jordan is, I have heard him say that there are times when he is so focused that it seems like time slows down. You hear that a lot with an athlete like him. Either he will say it or his opponents will say something like he is playing at a different speed, the game slows down for him, all of those kinds of things. I have studied consciousness for a long time, and I think that—like a lot of people, though not everybody, there is still debate about this—but consciousness is a series of discrete events, discrete frames. It doesn't appear to be discrete frames, it appears to be continuous, but think of it like a movie. A movie appears continuous, too, but in fact it is discrete frames, occurring at about 30 Hz,[1] that is where you lose the jitteriness.

---

[1] Hertz is a unit of frequency per second.

Most people have a baseline of about 40 Hz, as a marker of a constant—you have about 40 conscious instances per second. It can be a range, from 30–90. When you are drowsy it is slower and when you are excited it is faster. But most people, their rate of conscious moments at a normal part of their lives is going to be 40 Hz. People who are in a car accident, they might say that everything seemed to be in slow motion, and that is because they are excited, they are stimulated, so they are having more conscious moments per second. Everything slows down.

When you think about that and then you hear Michael Jordan say that when he was playing at certain times, it was like everything was in slow motion—the defense was in slow motion—what is likely happening is he is having more conscious moments per second than the defense. If the defense stays at 40 Hz, and Michael Jordan is able to raise his consciousness up to 80 Hz, he is seeing twice as much as the other players and is able to process that much more. He is able to make twice as many conscious decisions as his opponents. It is a natural thing; I have been saying that about athletes like him for years now.

The question is whether a player like Michael Jordan can train himself to do that, to raise his focus and see the game slow down. I think it is a matter of experience. By practicing at a certain level or being in certain situations again and again, you can probably get your-self to a certain level. That is certainly something that you saw over and over in Michael Jordan's career, and great athletes seem to have that possibility. There is no definitive answer to that, but if you see consciousness in terms of these discrete events that play out in front of you, it seems to be what happens with players like that. And if anyone has shown the ability to slow his game down at the critical moments, it has been Michael Jordan.

Charles Barkley

Forward

Career: 1985–2000

Career Highlights: ....10-time All-Star, 1991 All-Star Game MVP, 1993 NBA MVP, Inducted into the Naismith Memorial Basketball Hall of Fame (2006), NBA 50th Anniversary All-Time Team, two-time Olympic Gold Medalist

Jordan Highlights: .... Gold Medal in 1992 Olympics

Michael Jordan vs. Charles Barkley										
Regular Season	Games	Wins	Losses	Win %	Field Goal %	PPG	Points (High)	RPG	APG	SPG
Jordan	39	19	20	48.7	61.1	34.4	49 (twice)	5.7	5.9	3.1
Barkley	39	20	19	51.3	54.1	23.1	40 (1/30/87)	11.7	3.6	2.3

Playoffs	Games	Wins	Losses	Win %	Field Goal %	PPG	Points (High)	RPG	APG	SPG
Jordan	16	12	4	75.0	51.5	39.3	55 (6/16/93)	7.8	7.1	2.4
Barkley	16	4	12	25.0	53.6	25.7	42 (6/11/93)	13.4	5.3	1.1

A fellow 1984 draftee and Hall of Famer, Barkley was never able to win a championship, facing Jordan in the 1993 Finals when he was with the Suns—the same year Barkley was named league MVP. Barkley remains good friends with Jordan, which means he is still in constant competition with him.

THE THING ABOUT Michael Jordan is, he does not like to lose at anything. No matter what it is, on the basketball court, playing golf, cards, I don't care, that is what he is all about—winning. That's what sports are: it's competition. I mean, that's all it is. You're competing against other people. That's how it always is with Michael, he is always competing at everything. He is the most competitive person I ever met in my life.

We came up together. I got to know him back in 1984 when we were trying out for the Olympic team. It was an honor and privilege to be part of that 1984 draft and to be a player from that era. We had some great players who came up together, guys like John Stockton and Michael and Karl Malone, [Hakeem] Olajuwon, Patrick Ewing. That was a great time for the NBA. Unfortunately, we could not all win championships, because Michael and the Bulls were winning them all. But I don't consider losing to Michael Jordan, the greatest player in NBA history, to be anything that you should be ashamed of. He was that good. And it was not just him. I look at it like, there was Magic Johnson and Larry Bird, so you could lose to the Celtics or the Lakers just as easy. Magic, Michael, and Larry, you had three of the 10 greatest players ever on the floor, that was not a bad era to be part of.

I look at it like, hey, it would have been great to win a championship. I thought some of the teams I was on, in Phoenix and in Houston, that we had a chance. But we just were not good enough. But, looking back, losing to the Bulls and Michael Jordan, I don't think you can go crazy over that.

Jordan went against present and future Hall of Famers throughout his career. No matter the game, Jordan always showed up, but had a little extra in the tank against the best players in the league.

Dominique Wilkins

I remember a game he got 60 points against us, that was pretty impressive, but I think we won that at game.[2]

---

[2] The game was on April 16, 1987, and the Hawks won the game, 117–114.

He came at you from many different phases of the game. He was really good at getting inside your head. And if he got in your head, you were dead, done stick a fork in you, it was over.

We had respect for each other. He knew I was a serious competitor, and I knew he was a serious competitor. He never said much to me while we were playing, but I heard him talk to others. He didn't talk to me because he knew when a guy talked to me, I took it personally and would come back harder at you. We played different positions, so we weren't one-on-one much. He guarded me more than I guarded him.

The way he scored, you will never see a guy like that again. I feel very comfortable saying that: ever. There will never be another Michael Jordan.

I feel like I was in a slightly different era because he came into the league a few years after me. But I think playing Michael allowed you to measure how good you were. And I felt better about my abilities because I was able to play against him and succeed.

Even longtime Hawk Cliff Levingston remembers the battles between Jordan and Wilkins.

When I was with the Hawks, he and Dominique would have epic battles. Michael would come down and score, Dominique would go down and score. It was tit for tat between those two. If we were playing in Atlanta, Dominique would tell MJ, "You are not going to outshine me." Then when we came to Chicago, we would let Michael get his and stop everybody else. We usually won the game.

We were in Atlanta once, and Michael got the ball in the left corner. I was running out to close out on him, and he put the ball right in my face. I fell back, and he went by me and dunked the ball on Tree Rollins.

Kobe Bryant

Playing against him for the first time at the United Center, I felt like I was being thrown into the fire. He looked at me, and he made a baseline spin move and I knew it was coming. But he was so strong, by the time I tried to body him, he swatted me away like a fly.[3]

---

[3] This game, which took place on December 17, 1996, was before Kobe was a full-time starter. In ten minutes of play, Kobe scored five points, while Jordan racked up 30 points and nine rebounds in forty-seven minutes.

Avery Johnson

Guard

NBA Career: 1989–2004
Head Coaching Career: 2005–08, 2011–13
Career Highlights: .... 1999 NBA Finals Champion, 2006
Coach of the Year

Michael Jordan vs. Avery Johnson										
Regular Season	Games	Wins	Losses	Win %	Field Goal %	PPG	Points (High)	RPG	APG	SPG
Jordan	13	9	4	69.2	45.2	31.2	42 (1/24/93)	6.5	5.7	3.0
Johnson	13	4	9	30.8	41.8	8.2	23 (11/30/96)	1.7	4.9	0.5

The diminutive Johnson played 16 seasons in the NBA, mostly with the Spurs, where he teamed with greats like Tim Duncan and David Robinson (and, hint-hint, also with shooting guard Vinny Del Negro). He would go on to be the head coach of the Mavericks and Nets.

MICHAEL JORDAN WAS, in my mind, the most underpaid player in our game. Go back and look; whatever the salary cap was at that time in those days, he should have gotten all of it. He deserved it. He's the most fierce competitor on both ends of the floor I've ever seen in my life. He always came through: on the biggest stages at the biggest moments, the clutch situations. He was relentless, too. If he found a weakness he was going to keep going at it.

What probably gets overlooked with him, because he was so talented, is that he had a high, high, high basketball IQ. He always knew how to think out there, to get every advantage. Greatest player ever. He was the greatest, no doubt about it. I can't say anything more than that.

I do have a favorite memory playing against Michael Jordan, though. I would say it was one game when I was with the Spurs and they were coming in to play us. Bob Hill was our coach at the time. That day, Coach Hill jokingly told the two-guard—whose name I won't mention, I will keep him out of it—that he's not going to guard Michael. Hill said, "Avery is going to defend Michael." And the two-guard in question didn't say anything. I was listening and I was thinking that the coach was just joking.

So that morning, we go through shootaround, and we are planning out how we are going to play defense, and Coach Hill has not changed anything—I'm still guarding Michael Jordan. And then we got into our pregame routine and, it was still the same. You know, "Avery, you're going to defend Michael Jordan tonight," and the other guy, the two-guard, is going to guard Ron Harper or somebody. I was still not sure he was serious.

So, I started the game off and there I was, guarding Michael Jordan. I am not even six feet, and I am guarding Michael, who is 6-6.[4] And he looked at me on the first play of the game; it was like he was offended. I can't tell you exactly how he said it, for language reasons, but the clean version is: "What the heck are you guarding me for? Is this a joke?"

He proceeded to score a gazillion points on us. But I had a pretty good game, too.

---

[4] Johnson is listed at 5-10.

Eric Musselman

Head Coaching Career: 2003–2004, 2007

Musselman has been in coaching most of his adult life, serving as head coach of the Warriors and Kings, as well as an assistant to his father, the late Bill Musselman in Minnesota, and with Chuck Daly in Orlando in the late '90s.

WHEN I FIRST started coaching in Minnesota, we were still an expansion team but we figured the best way to approach him was to really try to go at him—he was a great defensive player, too, but we figured if you could wear him out by making him play defense, you could get into his legs a little bit and tire him out. It didn't necessarily work, but you just wanted him to have to guard as many possessions as possible. Wear him down as much as you could by not letting him get any rest on the defensive end.

But that can wear your guys down, too, and the big thing with playing against him is at the end of games, you had to be so precise defensively because of his ability to close games. In those situations, you knew, he was almost never going to make a mistake. He might miss a shot if you're lucky, but he was going to get a good shot, he was going to get a shot on his own terms. Whatever game plan, whatever scheme you are running as coaches, you have to be as focused as he is during those late-game situations. Not just the player defending him, but all five guys, because he was a really good passer in those situations, too. Like I said, at the end of games, he was always going to make the right play and get the shot that he wanted, either for himself or for his teammate so you could not lose your focus at all.

When I was with Coach [Chuck] Daly in Orlando in the late '90s. he would talk about it all the time with Michael, going back to their battles when he was in Detroit. He would tell stories all the time about how, in those playoff series, your late-game execution—on both sides of the ball—had to be so phenomenal because he put such pressure on you as a closer. That's why you'd try to make him defend during the game so that, at the end of the game, maybe there is a little less left in his tank. But he usually found a way to close out games, both offensively and defensively. He could make shots—even if their offensive sets broke down—he could still find a way to get the look he wanted. If you were going to beat them, you had to have a cushion. Some games you tell your team, "Keep it close, we can win it at the end." Against Jordan and those Bulls, it was more like, "We have got to have a cushion."

I remember when we played them [in 1997], Michael was thirty-five years old and he went out and he scored 29 points, but what was incredible was that he had 17 rebounds. And I was sitting behind the bench in that game, and Chuck is just continually looking back and saying, "Basketball genius. Basketball genius." That was one of his favorite things he would say about him. Or, Chuck would just go, "He's bionic, he's bionic, he's bionic," to no one in particular. He would just say it over and over. Or, "He runs on batteries." He always had these one-thought bullet points, and those three things were the ones he would say all the time with Jordan—bionic, runs on batteries, basketball genius. "We can't figure out what to do with this guy, he's a basketball genius, doesn't matter what we do."

Chuck had a special bond with any of those guys who were on the Dream Team, especially Michael. He had a special admiration for him because of the way he carried himself and the way he approached the game. The competitiveness he had, even in practice. Chuck would tell stories more about the practices they had with the Dream Team than the games themselves. They went at each other pretty hard. He would always talk in team meetings about the guys in the NBA at the time and how they had no idea how hard those players on the Dream Team pushed themselves, even knowing they knew they were going to go out and win every game by 50—how hard Jordan pushed everybody, almost pulled them, willed them from a competitive standpoint.

There is no question he is the best I have seen, the best I have coached against. No offense to LeBron James or Dwyane Wade or Kobe Bryant, guys you have to put together a game plan against. I would say he is number one, and probably Kobe number two. That would be my order, because Jordan was able to do so much. Not just scoring, but defense, passing, rebounding. He kept improving his shot, his range out to the perimeter. And the big thing: his post-up midrange game. That takes a lot of work, and it was obviously something he was willing to work on, even as he got into his thirties. A lot of that had to do with the stories you hear about him lifting weights in the morning, the pride he took in conditioning. He was someone who was way ahead of everyone else in that sense.

That is why Coach Daly used that bionic term. Because of his ability to sustain greatness, mentally and physically—he was almost limitless as far as age goes.

Grant Long

Forward

Michael Jordan vs. Grant Long										
Regular Season	Games	Wins	Losses	Win %	Field Goal %	PPG	Points (High)	RPG	APG	SPG
Jordan	28	26	2	92.8	53.4	29.6	47 (4/1/90)	6.1	5.6	2.0
Long	28	2	26	7.2	43.4	9.0	21 (12/2/89)	6.2	2.0	0.9
Playoffs	Games	Wins	Losses	Win %	Field Goal %	PPG	Points (High)	RPG	APG	SPG
Jordan	3	3	0	100	60.9	45.0	56 (4/29/92)	9.7	6.7	3.0
Long	3	0	3	0.0	41.7	12.3	17 (4/29/92)	5.0	2.7	1.7

Long played 15 seasons in the NBA, but started out as an original member of the Heat. Jordan seemed to have a special affinity for playing against Miami, and according to Long, that might have been rooted in some ill-advised trash talk by a teammate.

I WAS IN MIAMI from the beginning, when the Heat were an expansion team in 1988. And the team we could not beat was the Bulls. We lost to them 19 times in a row before we finally beat them.[5] They were always focused when they played against us.

I have to go back and say, Michael probably had a reason for

---

[5] Three of those 19 losses include the Bulls sweeping the Heat in the first round of the '92 playoffs.

that. At that time, both teams, at halftime, would go through the same corridor under the stadium to get to their locker rooms. There was one particular game, it was in 1990, and Michael had only 10 or 12, if that, at halftime. One of our players, Willie Burton, was guarding him for a few possessions and had blocked one of Michael's shots. So in the tunnel, he is bragging about that, saying, "I'm shutting him down. I got him on lockdown. I am locking him down."

Willie did not know it, but Michael is about three feet behind him and is hearing all this. Willie had not even played all that much in the game, but he had to guard Michael a little. And, you have to understand, Willie was one of those guys who just talked all the time. It was part of who he was. So he's running his mouth a little bit heading in for halftime, and that was all Michael needed to hear.

We come out at halftime and Michael motions to me and Steve Smith. He calls us over to the center circle and says, "I have had a cold for a while, I have not been feeling great. But your buddy over there was talking smack, so now I am about to turn it up on you all." He motioned to Willie. Then I think he scored 37 in the second half and they went on to win the game.[6] After the game, me and Steve were like, "Willie, man, why did you have to open your big mouth?" But there was nothing you could do about it. When you are looking at this guy and you see that he is capable of doing that, there is nothing you can do to knock him out.

The time we finally broke that streak, the 19-game losing streak, it was the day before my birthday, I remember it well. Michael was playing, and we were very, very excited. It was like, *Can you believe this? We are going to beat the Chicago Bulls!* I remember it was Steve Smith who actually made some big shots down the stretch to help us win that game, and Michael just missed some shots at the end. He was going to the rim at the end of the game with a chance to tie it, but he just missed. It was an incredible feeling because they were having a

---

[6] Jordan totaled 47 points to beat the Heat, 111–103, on April 1, 1990.

dominant year and the fact we beat them was just a blip on the radar, but for us it was a big deal.

I remember playing them in that first playoff series. We had never been in the postseason before, and we did not really come storming into the playoffs, we had backed into them. We lost our last game, but we would still get in if someone else in the East would lose on the last night of the year.[7] There were six or seven guys at my house watching their game, and when they wound up losing, we were just ecstatic. We were not even thinking, *Wait, we have got to play the Bulls?* But that was our prize.

It was still great. That my first experience of playoff basketball and what it was like. I thought the fans had done a great job of supporting us throughout the year, but in the playoffs it was just a whole different level, especially because it was Michael Jordan and the Bulls. It was a different level of support and energy in that building, even though we lost the first two games in Chicago. We got out there in Miami for Game 3, and we were ahead by 16, 17 points. We were hitting every shot, we were moving the ball, one step ahead of them, I was catching alley-oop passes and dunking, we were high-fiving each other all over the place. And Michael was not doing much of anything.[8]

But once we got over that initial burst of energy, the Chicago Bulls, the veteran team, they sort of said, "Okay, you guys done having your fun now? Go sit down." And they turned it on. Now, I have played a lot of playoff basketball since then, so I know that first home game against a playoff team, there is a lot of energy in the building and the team can feed off that. But if you can withstand that first run from the home team, you will have a chance to settle back into a groove and play your game. But we were a young team so we tried to ride

---

[7] In 1992, both Atlanta and Miami finished the regular season tied at 38–44, but the Heat held the tiebreaker advantage.

[8] Jordan did not score in the first ten minutes, and the Heat led by as many as 18 points.

that emotion throughout the game, but you can't do that over the whole forty-eight minutes. At some point, you are going to come down and you have got to play basketball. We did not understand that. The Bulls did.

Once things settled down, they were just waiting on us. That is when they took over. Michael especially. He started so slow but he went out and put 56 points on us. He kidded about it after the game, about why he started slow. He said he had played 36 holes of golf before the game. How can a guy be that good after playing 36 holes of golf in the Florida sun? I don't even think he was that good of a golfer at that time, so he had to be out there struggling. But he played 36 holes and still kicked our butts.

Steve Smith
Guard

Career: 1992–2005
Career Highlights: .. 1998 All-Star, 2003 NBA Finals Champion

Michael Jordan vs. Steve Smith										
Regular Season	Games	Wins	Losses	Win %	Field Goal %	PPG	Points (High)	RPG	APG	SPG
Jordan	18	13	5	72.2	49.9	28.1	47 (12/27/97)	5.2	4.2	1.1
Smith	18	5	13	27.8	39.2	16.6	26 (2/13/98)	4.6	2.2	0.9

Playoffs	Games	Wins	Losses	Win %	Field Goal %	PPG	Points (High)	RPG	APG	SPG
Jordan	8	7	1	87.5	51.9	33.5	56 (4/29/92)	10.0	5.8	2.4
Smith	8	1	7	12.5	38.7	17.0	27 (5/8/97)	2.4	2.9	0.8

Smith was the fifth pick in the 1991 draft, going to the Heat, a team that had only been founded in 1988. He would go on to have a long history guarding Jordan in his 14-year career, but as a rookie, he helped Miami to its first-ever NBA playoff berth—and it did not end well for the Heat.

THE THING THAT stands out most is that, I remember the sort of education Michael gave me in my first year.[9] We had a lot of respect for each other. We would trash talk a little, but mostly we had respect for each other.

---

[9] Smith was a rookie with the Miami Heat in 1991.

I played against Jordan during an exhibition [before the season started]; we had the Hall of Fame game in Springfield, Massachusetts. We did not have our usual point guard, Sherman Douglas, so I had to handle the ball a lot. And when you are going against Michael Jordan and Scottie Pippen and the rest of those guys—even in an exhibition season—that is not a fun thing to have to do. I think we held our own, but they made sure they beat us. It was an exhibition, but they were there to win.[10]

That year, we actually made the playoffs for the first time ever; Miami was still a new franchise and we were maybe four years in and got to the postseason. And, okay, great, we are in the playoffs. But we were the eighth seed. Now we have to play the Bulls, as they were the first seed. They had just won the year before, so this was when Mike was really at his peak. But we were young and were kind of like a team that had nothing to lose. What I did not understand at the time is that things change in the playoffs. If you go back to the Michael Jordan we saw in that exhibition game, he wanted to win. We saw them in the season, he wanted to win. But in the playoffs, he was just different.

Michael took over, the Bulls took over. I did pretty well that first game, I had 19 points, and we were actually winning early in the game. I was talking a little bit to Michael, Glen Rice was talking. But then they just changed and took the game over. Michael was just doing everything: he was scoring, passing, rebounding, he almost had a triple-double.[11] And they just kept coming. Then, the third game, the final game—it (the first round) was only a best of five then—there was a rumor that he had been playing golf [that day]. He did not score much in the first quarter, so of course, we were thinking maybe he was tired, maybe because of the golfing. But then he went out and put up 56 points. Most of that was on me, too.

---

[10] Chicago won the game, 124–118.
[11] Jordan finished the game with 46 points, 11 rebounds, and nine assists.

It taught me a lot. I tell young players that all the time now, going up against the best is one thing, but going up against the best in a playoff series is totally different. It is such a different atmosphere; such a different level of basketball. It is the NBA, but it's another level. The level of commitment from those guys, the level of commitment throughout the game, it was amazing. We were young, so we kind of played in spurts. But to see great players consistently play at a certain level, I think that is what I learned from that.

That's what I took from that [series] for my whole career. For me, playing that guy, Michael Jordan, it was such a learning experience.

When the Bulls went against Smith's Hawks in the 1997 Eastern Conference Semifinals, he was quoted as saying that "guarding Michael [Jordan] is easy." He was able to clarify that statement for us.

I got a lot of heat for that. But what I meant was that Michael did not run through a lot of screens to get open. He was trickier than that. He would stand still and wait for something to open up. He knew once he got the ball, he was going to be dangerous, no matter where he was on the floor. Sometimes he would make a quick move once he got the ball, but more often he liked to see the defender get set in front of him, then break that guy down. The one thing I knew was that he was always thinking, trying to figure out which way to go, and what move would break you.

Antonio Harvey

Forward

Career: **1994–2003**

| Michael Jordan vs. Antonio Harvey | | | | | | | | | | |
Regular Season	Games	Wins	Losses	Win %	Field Goal %	PPG	Points (High)	RPG	APG	SPG
Jordan	2	2	0	100	48.8	25.0	29 (11/30/95)	6.0	5.0	2.5
Harvey	2	0	2	0.0	50.0	7.0	9 (11/30/95)	5.0	0.5	0.5

Harvey was a forward who played 10 professional seasons, with six NBA teams. He was a member of the Lakers originally, but was selected by the Grizzlies in the expansion draft in 1995 and was on the floor when newly established Vancouver nearly upset the powerhouse Bulls (emphasis on nearly).

MICHAEL JORDAN WAS my idol. Going through high school and into college, all my friends knew, I had Michael Jordan posters on the wall and all of that. He was retired, though, my first two years in the league, playing baseball for those two seasons. He actually came back from his retirement during my second year, but it was right after we faced Chicago for the last time that season. So I was two years into my career and I never got to play against him. But yes, finally, with the Grizzlies in Vancouver in 1995, I got to play against him for the first time, and it was maybe my all-time favorite moment in the NBA. Just because it was Michael Jordan. For me, that was the utmost.

I remember it well. We were playing in Vancouver, and he was having a real tough night. I think he was 4-for-15 from the field, he had only 10 points, and he sat out most of the third quarter. Just a really poor night for a player like Michael Jordan. We came from behind, and we were winning the game in the fourth quarter. Now, this was the Bulls team that went on to win 72 games, so this was a little bit of a shock. We were an expansion team, it was our first season. We won 15 games that year—everyone was there to see Jordan, not us. But our fans were really into the game, they were giving us a standing ovation because it looked like we were actually going to win. It was a really cool moment for a team that was supposed to be as bad as us.

But one of our guards at the time, Darrick Martin, had been with Michael Jordan during the summer. He was one of the guys in the movie *Space Jam*, working out with Mike at Warner Bros. The long and short of it is, Darrick thought they were kind of like friends because of the movie, because they had hung out during the summer and Darrick thought that meant he could talk trash. So—I have to clean it up, I can't tell you what was said word-for-word—but Darrick started yelling, "Aw, Mike, it's just not falling tonight, Mike!" And he ran by their bench and yelled, "I told you we were going to beat you, Mike!"

Halfway through the fourth quarter, we have the lead by eight points or so. Michael is listening to Darrick, and finally, he gets up and checks back into the game. He proceeded to score, I think it was 20 points in a row, in just a few minutes.[12] He was doing it all—he was posting up, he was driving to the basket, he was dunking. I felt bad for Byron Scott, who was trying to guard him. And Byron was at the end of his career, thirty-four or thirty-five years old, trying to keep up with Michael Jordan. And Michael was playing angry, which is not a good thing if you're guarding him.

---

[12] Jordan scored 19 points in a six-minute span.

Michael hit a fadeaway, falling toward our bench. After it went in, he went and leaned down in front of Darrick Martin and said, "Shut up, you little [expletive]!"

After the game, Byron Scott comes into the locker room and you could tell he was heated, he was not happy with the way that game ended. We had a chance to win a big game on our home floor. So it was quiet, and he turns to Darrick and says, "Hey, man, do me a favor. Don't talk [expletive] to my guy. Reserve that stuff for your guy." Oh, it was something else. It was maybe the greatest performance I have ever seen firsthand, it was that good. Even now, there are clips of that game on YouTube, that is how good it was.

But that was the thing you learned from playing against him. You can't give him any motivation. There was a story about a guy at the time, he played for Washington—LaBradford Smith. He came out one night and had a huge game, he had like 40 points against Michael one night and as they were coming off the court, he patted Michael on the back and kind of sarcastically said, "Nice game, Mike." You know, like, better luck next time. And Mike did have better luck next time, because he scored 47 points the next time out against LaBradford Smith, and most of those were in the first half.[13]

The lesson was: you don't talk to Mike. You hope that Mike is having a bad night, and if he is, then you sit quietly and be happy about it. Too many people have gotten stung by celebrating a little too much when they beat Michael. Don't poke the bear. Avoid the bear at all costs.

[13] Jordan later confessed that he fabricated the part about LaBradford Smith saying, "Nice game, Mike," in media interviews. The games in question took place as part of a back-to-back in March 1993. Smith had just scored 37 points on Jordan, and Jordan wanted to use that output as motivation, because the Bulls were playing the Bullets the next night. He included the made-up taunt by Smith as an extra boost—but the legend remains, even among players of that era.

Will Perdue

Center

Career: 1989–2001
Career Highlights: ....four-time NBA Finals Champion
Jordan Highlights: Won three NBA Finals with Jordan (1991–93)

Michael Jordan vs. Will Perdue										
Regular Season	Games	Wins	Losses	Win %	Field Goal %	PPG	Points (High)	RPG	APG	SPG
Jordan	6	6	0	100	43.6	29.3	28 (11/22/95)	7.2	3.7	2.7
Perdue	6	0	6	0.0	44.4	3.5	9 (11/30/96)	7.3	0.0	0.3

Perdue was one of many centers Bulls general manager Jerry Krause brought into the team in hopes of finding someone Jordan could play with, but Jordan mostly considered centers as players who just got in his way. Perdue played behind Bill Cartwright most of his career with the Bulls, then was traded by the team in the summer of 1995 to bring Dennis Rodman over from San Antonio. That gave Perdue the chance to play against Jordan.

THIS WASN'T WHEN I was playing against him, but I remember when I was his teammate and we were playing the Washington Wizards, except they were the Bullets at the time. They had a player named LaBradford Smith, who was a couple of years into the league, and I think it was 1992 or 1993 that Smith had a big night playing against Michael. I forget how many he scored, but it was a lot.[14] That was his career high. I don't know if we won or lost the game,[15] but I remember that somebody made a big deal out of it. I would guess the Bullets did. But that was a mistake, because the schedule had us playing the Bullets the next night in Chicago in a back-to-back home-and-road deal. I remember Michael told everybody he was going to get 37 in the first half against Smith the next night. Before the game, I think it was John Paxson who told me to "get out of his way." Whatever Smith had in that first game, Michael matched him in the first half of the second game.[16] It was the best example of how competitive he was, and that was what made him so good.

He was so competitive in practice, but he would only talk to us on the second team when he was trying to motivate himself. I remember that he walked out of practice at least twice because he felt the coaches weren't being fair in how they called scrimmages, giving advantages to us as we tried to play hard against him.

I used to do this drill with our trainers on rebounding it was all about getting off the floor quick, put backs, second chance opportunities, and I remember Michael would get mad that I would never bring the ball to the floor and that is when he liked to steal the ball from the big guys when they brought the ball down to his level.

Even some teammates of Jordan went against him before joining the Bulls.

Bill Wennington (won two rings with Jordan)

I was with the Sacramento Kings when we were playing the Bulls in 1991, and they ran a high screen roll with Bill Cartwright.

---

[14] Jordan had 37 points on 15-of-20 shooting.
[15] The Bulls won, 104–99.
[16] Actually, Jordan only got 36 in the first half of the second game.

I switched onto Michael. So I'm doing a great job, I'm sliding my feet, and even though I know I'm going up against the greatest player in the NBA, I feel I am doing a decent job. He starts backpedaling, and I'm thinking, "That's right, I'm making Michael Jordan back up," and then all of a sudden, just shoots a bullet pass past me to Cartwright under the basket. He was pulling me further and further away from the post. I thought I was doing a good thing but I wasn't.

Toni Kukoc (won three rings with Jordan)

Speaking of going against Jordan during the 1992 Olympics, after he had just been drafted by the Bulls.

It was hard to run, even across half court without the ball. Even when I had the ball, I was looking around saying, "Someone come get this." I had questions from my teammates during the game. They were asking me, "What is going on? Do you not see that they are trying to get you off the court?" I told them then, "I guess that is how the NBA game is played."

Randy Brown (won three rings with Jordan)

I was in Sacramento—the season before I signed to join the Bulls—and I was given the assignment of guarding Michael Jordan after Mitch Richmond, so I had to take him after Mitch needed a blow. I remember looking at [Coach] Garry St. Jean and I said, "Are you serious?" It was a great challenge. After being in awe of him for so many years, after the first couple of minutes of guarding him, I kind of got the competitive drive because I saw he was such a competitor that it drove me to ask to become a Bull. I guess I wanted to be like Mike. Guarding him kind of led me to being a Bull the following year.

I'm about five inches shorter than Mike, so when I guarded him, he took me down to the post. I knew I wasn't very good, so if I didn't play hard, if I didn't pressure, he was going to get the best of me. I remember Michael was at the top of the triangle, and I was pressuring him, and of course I remember Phil Jackson calling out of his favorite plays right to the post, one of those snapback plays. I know all those plays now. But Michael took me into the post and shot right over me. I fouled him, because that was all I could do.

I guarded him almost every day in practice, and one thing I learned from him was when he would say, "It's never going to get any tougher than this." And it didn't. He and Scottie were the first to ever teach me about guarding angles. I thought I was a good defender until I got with those guys. They showed me the way a little bit, showed me to be a better defender, because I didn't know anything about angles until I got here.

Darrell Walker (won one ring with Jordan)

I remember how tough a cover he was, how smart a basketball player he was. People get caught up about how much talent he had, but nobody talked about his intelligence. You had to come with your A-game defensively just to contain him a little bit. We had some battles over the years, I always looked forward when we'd go to Chicago or when they'd come to Washington when I was with the Bullets. Coach Wes Unseld would always say in our pregame meetings: "Darrell, you have MJ, and we are not coming to help you." That's the way it was, and I accepted that challenge. It was a pleasure to compete against him. He has been underrated as a defender his whole career, even though he did make the All-Defensive teams a number of times.

He was never mouthy with me. We would just battle. I remember B. J. Armstrong told me years later, when I was with the Bulls, that whenever Chicago was getting ready to play Washington, Michael would say, "I have to deal with that damn Darrell Walker tonight." That was a compliment.

When I came to play for the Bulls, I guarded him in every practice. He practiced just as hard as he played—maybe harder—so the game was so much easier for him. One time in practice, we were really going at it, I mean really going at it, and [Coach] Phil [Jackson] said, "You two stop," and MJ said, "Don't worry about us. You worry about everybody else."

Jim Barnett

Career: **1967–77**

Barnett played 11 seasons in the NBA, facing one of the players Jordan has always said he'd like to go against in a game: Lakers legend Jerry West. As a broadcaster, Barnett has been courtside for the Warriors for more than three decades.

THERE WAS A game where we were playing against the Bulls on our home floor, and as you know, you could not give Michael Jordan anything to motivate him. This was when the Bulls were winning championships still, when they were at their peak. And it was Latrell Sprewell who said something about how good of a scorer he was, that he could score with Michael Jordan. And I remember, the first half—this is a fact—Latrell Sprewell had two points the entire half. Michael Jordan was all over him, like a glove. And the only reason Sprewell had those two points was because he cherry-picked a layup at one end—he did not run back on defense one time and somehow the ball got turned over—so he was standing alone on the offensive end. They got a pass to him and he laid it in. Those were his only two points and, otherwise, he would not have scored a point in that half. The Bulls were up by something like 30 points at halftime.

Jordan absolutely shut down Sprewell that night, and if you look, he did that pretty consistently, at least when Sprewell was in Golden State.[17] But that is how he was. He used things like that to motivate him if he saw someone say something about him—whether it was misconstrued or whether it was made up—he would take that and use it throughout his whole career any time he saw the guy. He was that way with Sprewell. He was just so competitive.

I remember, John Bach, who was an assistant with Doug Collins in Chicago early on in Michael's career, he used to tell me these stories about how Michael would play in practice. They would draft a guy and he would come in as a rookie and Michael would go up against him. Michael would go at the rookie and practice and just beat him every time, try to not let him score. So John Bach went up to him and said, "Michael, you are killing this guy in practice. You have got to take it easy on him. I am trying to build up his confidence, and you are destroying him." It wasn't only physically on the court, it was verbally, too. John told him, "You have got to stop doing that to all our new players." But he took no prisoners.

Everybody remembers the big shots he made, the shot against Craig Ehlo or the one against Bryon Russell, but I think the most interesting thing about him is that he quit in the middle of his career and went to play baseball. As a player, I could not even fathom that, quitting in the middle of your career and just deciding you're going to go play another sport. But he is a guy who likes challenges. If people say, "You can't do that," he is going to want to do that. And quite frankly, I thought he did pretty damn well out there for someone who was just trying to pick up baseball at that stage of his life.

---

[17] Jordan outscored Sprewell by nearly 10 points a game, and the Bulls were 5–0 against the Warriors during Sprewell's six seasons there.

He is the quintessential athlete and competitor who can motivate himself to a level that a normal person just can't get to. He understood what it was and how to get himself there, and how to be at his best every night. A lot of people didn't like that, because you are going to rub some people the wrong way when you do that. Even himself, he was extremely hard on himself. He would have games where he had 43 points, and he would say after, "I should have had 50." He was thinking about the shots he missed or the free throws or whatever.

The one player I came across in my career who had that same trait, that same ability to motivate himself the way Michael did, was Jerry West. He had that. Jerry West only played well against good competition, and only if he was challenged. If he was not challenged and the guy he was playing against was inferior, it was hard for him to be at his peak. The best was brought out of him by people who made it hard on him, and that is when he would rise to the challenge. He was always better in playoff games. In 1965, the Lakers played the Baltimore Bullets to go to the Finals. Elgin Baylor got hurt, and I believe it was six games, and Jerry averaged 45 points a game in that series.[18] Because he knew he had to pick up the slack because Elgin was not there.

Jerry West and Michael Jordan, those were the two guys who were able to do that unlike anyone else I have ever seen—block out everything else, no distractions, nothing from the outside would get in once they were playing in a game. It was like they were in a gym playing one-on-one with someone, with no crowd there, not even with other players there. That level of focus has got to be very difficult to accomplish, but they were able to do it. They're special that way.

---

[18] West averaged 46.3 per game that series.

Section Five: Legacy

"When you look at the league and where it is now, where the Finals are and all the fans of the game that we have in this country and globally, it is obviously a part of the Michael Jordan legacy of being one of the first athletes to really take this game to new heights."

—Miami Heat guard, Dwyane Wade

IN THE END, folks around the NBA wound up doing the right thing—after Jordan retired from the Bulls in 1998 (then came back briefly with the Wizards), it seemed that the league was on an endless hunt for the "next Michael Jordan," relentlessly attempting to fit up-and-coming players into Jordan's too-big mold. The NBA finally gave up on that and instead simply allowed its next wave of stars to establish itself and its own identity.

In the meantime, NBA fans—new and old—can simply appreciate Jordan for all he accomplished within the game and the way he helped elevate basketball to global popularity. An entire generation of sports fans in this country was raised knowing Jordan as the best and most popular athlete on the planet, and rather than searching for a player who can duplicate that, we now let Jordan's legacy stand on its own.

That is what this final section deals with—the lasting impact Michael Jordan's career had on the young players he came across in the NBA, those still in the NBA and even one Chicagoan just now entering the league. Jordan's greatness remains unmatched, his stardom secure and his legacy well worth the celebration it receives.

Mike Fratello

Head Coaching Career: .. 1981, 1984–90, 1994–99, 2005–07
Career Highlights: .... 1986 Coach of the Year

Known as "The Czar," Fratello coached 1,215 games in the NBA (winning 667 of them) and also is one of the league's most respected analysts, working now for NBA TV. His history with Jordan dates back to high school camps and includes his time as a coach at Jordan's annual fantasy camp.

I MET HIM AFTER his sophomore year in high school, he was at a Five-Star basketball camp. It must have been 1979. You saw this long athlete, very thin, skinny legs, but definitely a young man with some promise. You just hoped he was going to grow into those legs and arms. Because you could tell, he was smooth, he would kind of glide down the floor as he ran. He was very smooth and you thought, *There could maybe be something special there.*

Here we are, thirty-five years later, and I think his impact is still being felt, in the NBA and in all of sports, really. The impact goes beyond him winning six championships with the Bulls and all the scoring that he did; the dunk contests he won and the success he had on the court. You can probably look as some type of indicator to how important he was to the game and what he meant to it by looking at the fact that still—even at this age for him—he still has a shoe brand that probably outsells everyone else's shoe brand on the market. That is pretty darn good for a guy who is fifty and has been out of the game for a long time now. Most players—even the great ones—are forgotten at that point. They don't go out and have people of all ages buying their sneakers every day. Not this guy, not Michael.

I think a lot of it goes back to his mom and dad and how they raised him—the kind of person he is. He always surrounded himself with smart, competent people. And then the guidance he got from David Falk, his agent, and how he handled himself in terms of the decisions they made over the years. He was very aware that everyone wanted a piece of him, but that doesn't mean you should say yes to everything. They were very careful about what endorsements to select and what not to select. Making *Space Jam*, for example, you appeal to the younger kids coming up in a different way, not just basketball. No one had done that before on the scale that Michael was doing it, with that level of consistent success.

He was just a basketball player at first, but he very much understood what it meant to really be a star, and not just a guy who could dunk. He had responsibilities because he was a global icon, and he carried himself that way. He was always professional and always someone who presented himself as a role model who could walk in front of a camera or a microphone and always handle himself the right way. Win or lose, he was going to be dressed well, he was going to be calm, he was going to face the music. It was a great job by the people around him and, of course, by him, to be able to pull it off, especially under the pressure he was under.

One game that really stands out, I was working with Marv Albert for NBC at the time, and it was the first game of the Finals in 1992, against the Blazers. That's the one where he came out and made all those 3-pointers in the first half. We had actually been talking to him before that, just the standard thing you do to prepare for a broadcast.

And he told us, he was going to make some 3s that day. He was not really a 3-point shooter, but he just sort of knew it.

It was an incredible display, of course. He started making those shots, and he just kept taking them. As you should—if you're making them, then keep shooting. The last one, Portland's Cliff Robinson was on him, he was playing him exactly like you want to, sort of standing back off him and taking away the dribble. But Michael just put it up and, it went right in. And Cliff looked up like he could not believe what was going on. And Michael turns to Marv and me and Magic [Johnson] at the broadcast table and just shrugs. It became one of those really memorable moments from his career.

Marv, to this day, wants everybody to think that it was him who Michael was looking at. I keep telling him, "It wasn't you, Marv; he was looking past you. He was looking at me." I was sitting on Marv's right-hand side. He doesn't want to believe me. If you want to know the truth, actually, what happened was, Jack Nicholson was to my right, because he was filming *Hoffa*, and he was in Chicago. He had wanted to come to the game, but the NBA had no tickets left for him. So they pulled a chair up next to our table and Jack sat right there.

Probably, it was Jack who Michael was shrugging toward. But Marv will still say it was him. I am sticking with me. Let's just say it is still a hotly debated topic.

A player's approach to the game (and Jordan) can also affect the outcome, as shown by the comments of Jason Kidd and O. J. Mayo.

Jason Kidd

The best player I played against has to be Michael Jordan, because of the expectation each night. I'm going to see Michael, what is he going to go for: 40, 50, 60? He never let down those people. He always came to put on a show. That made him one of the hardest guys to guard. He was on stage every night. He can get to the basket, he can jump over you, and he can hit the jump shot. He wasn't a guy who was quiet. He would talk a little trash, and that is putting it nicely.

The first time guarding him in Dallas, I was a little nervous. I think he could see that, and he told me, "Don't worry, kid, I won't embarrass you tonight." So I was guarding him right out of the box, and he did a spin move on the baseline and I said to myself don't dunk it, but he jumped up and just kept going. He went to the other side of the basket and did a layup. He winked at me and said, "I told you I wasn't going to embarrass you." He had 35 that game.

O. J. Mayo, who participated in Jordan's annual camp in 2006, when Mayo was the top-ranked high school player in the nation, shares what happened when he got a bit too cocky against Jordan.

O. J. Mayo

I happened to be the only high school player [participating at the camp]. It was mainly freshmen in college. So he came on the court and he guarded me. I thought *Man, he must think I am not the strong link here*. So I get it going a little bit. Obviously, it is any ballplayer's dream to play against Mike. I got a few buckets and I think the campers knew I was only a high school kid, and so they got rowdy a little bit. We played two team games—I think we split one and one. Then he told all the campers to leave. So we continued playing pickup, and Mike was being Mike. He was jawing a little bit and really getting into me defensively. He was backing me down when he had the ball. He said, "You better scream for momma." Then he hit the famous fadeaway on me. And then I said, "Okay, I see you got it going."

He said, "You may be the best high school player in the world, but I'm the greatest ever. Don't you ever disrespect the great like that."

Nick Van Exel

Guard

Career: 1994–2006
Career Highlights: ....1998 NBA All-Star

Michael Jordan vs. Nick Van Exel										
Regular Season	Games	Wins	Losses	Win %	Field Goal %	PPG	Points (High)	RPG	APG	SPG
Jordan	8	4	4	50.0	40.0	22.9	36 (12/17/96)	6.4	5.0	1.5
Exel	8	4	4	50.0	46.5	14.3	36 (12/17/97)	3.9	6.4	1.1

Nick Van Exel was one of those basketball players who grew into maturity watching Michael Jordan play for the Bulls, and when he got his chance to play against him, he looked forward to it with pleasure. After an exciting two-year career with the University of Cincinnati, Van Exel entered the NBA with the Los Angeles Lakers, serving as the replacement for Magic Johnson.

I REMEMBER A GAME when I was real young, just into the league (1993), and he made a move where he came in and out and then went to the left side and made a left-handed layup. It was an amazing move. I wanted to stop and get his autograph, but I couldn't because I was in the game. It was so memorable. It was so much like the famous move he made in the game against the Los Angeles Lakers in the 1991 playoffs, where he laid the ball up on the right side, but switched at the last second to the left side. When he did the same sort of thing against the Lakers and I was on the team, I had to stop and think: *I'm on the court with Michael Jordan.*

We always talked trash with each other, because I was a real trash talker. You know Michael would always talk trash. He and Scottie were both really good trash talkers. But it was kind of hard to really get into it with Michael because you knew he was always going to get all the calls. It was an unfair battle for me, but I didn't care, I was just happy to be out on the court with him. I just let him know I wasn't going to back down.

He tried to post me up all the time, because he was several inches taller than me. He would take me down, and he wouldn't bully me, he would just bump into me, then turn around and hit that fadeaway jump shot and run down the court with his tongue hanging out. He knew how to use his body. I was a smaller guard, and he knew he could jump over me at any time. It was just a regular jump shot for him when he was playing against me.

Dwyane Wade

Guard

Career: 2004–Present
Career Highlights: .... 10-time All-Star, three-time NBA Finals
Champion, 2006 NBA Finals MVP,
2010 All-Star Game MVP

Wade is a future Hall of Famer who has spent his entire career—which includes three championships—in Miami. But he grew up as a kid on Chicago's South Side, idolizing and emulating Jordan.

WHEN YOU LOOK at the league and where it is now, where the Finals are and all the fans of the game that we have in this country and globally, it is obviously a part of the Michael Jordan legacy as being one of the first athletes to really take this game to new heights.

And as a Bulls fan growing up, my first memory—my favorite memory—is probably the first championship they won [in 1991]. You just remember being proud for your city—knowing all the struggles that the Bulls went through at the time, not getting over the hump for so long, losing to Detroit two years in a row, and getting an opportunity to get to that first Finals versus the Lakers and against Magic Johnson. And for them to win that first championship, as a city, being in Chicago, I was proud.

189

That was when I was nine years old. That was a time when I really fell in love with the game of basketball. That was the time when I went out in the backyard, no matter what—cold outside, or wet, whatever it was—and I was trying to emulate Michael Jordan. Especially that move he did against the Lakers when he went up in the lane and decided he didn't want to dunk it, he wanted to go ahead and change it up, change hands in the air and shoot the whoop-de-whoop shot with his left hand. I tried that so many times.

I wasn't really fortunate enough when I was a kid to have a lot of [Bulls] stuff. My favorite thing about that time was just being in Chicago and being proud to be able to watch the Chicago Bulls on WGN, and the rest of the world could see them as much as me. That was my favorite thing; just to be proud to say I was a Chicago Bulls fan and Michael Jordan fan and that I lived in Chicago. I felt like it was personal; like I knew the guy. I didn't know him, but I just felt that way. It made me proud.

Even though MJ wasn't from Chicago, he made you feel like he was, just like a lot of kids think I'm from Miami when they're growing up. It just made you want to be that, you wanted to be great like that. You wanted to do some of the things off the court that he did. So when you went out in the backyard, when you went to the gym, you might watch the "Come and Fly with Me" video before you went—whatever you do—you are going out and you are emulating that person. You're imitating him. That's what a lot of us wanted to do.

That's what his legacy is and has been. It is just, now, you can see the impact that it played on my life and so many kids' lives at the time. Obviously I'm still benefitting from that today in the NBA.

Rashard Lewis

Forward

Career: 1999–Present
Career Highlights: ...... two-time All-Star, NBA Finals Champion

Michael Jordan vs. Rashard Lewis										
Regular Season	Games	Wins	Losses	Win %	Field Goal %	PPG	Points (High)	RPG	APG	SPG
Jordan	3	1	2	33.3	42.9	23.0	27 (11/12/02)	9.3	4.0	1.3
Lewis	3	2	1	66.7	52.0	21.7	37 (11/12/02)	7.0	1.3	0.7

Lewis, a Houston native, has played 16 seasons in the NBA, earning two All-Star berths and appearing in three different NBA Finals. He also played against Jordan during his Washington Wizards comeback, when Lewis was with the Sonics.

MICHAEL JORDAN CREATED the way for a lot of players today. You think about basketball, you think about Michael Jordan. He is going to be the first person that comes to most people's minds, even kids who are too young to have seen him. He pretty much changed the game in terms of the way we approach it as players, the way we present ourselves, doing media, all of those things. If you look back, he always had a suit and tie on. I think players here now, they want to present themselves that way. So you see the big stars like Kevin Durant and LeBron [James] and Dwyane Wade, they are conscious about things like that. That started with Michael Jordan. He was the consummate professional, and when you go back and look at film, you can see that he was always aware of that—he was always going to present himself that way, both on and off the court.

I was a fan of his growing up, just because of what he did for the league and how he lifted it up for everyone. I grew up in Houston, so I was always watching Hakeem Olajuwon. He was a center and I was tall, but I was not a center when I was a kid. I was playing on the wing. So I was paying attention to Michael and trying to do the things he would do.

I loved those Rockets teams in the mid-'90s, I was a kid then so watching them and seeing them win it all (in 1994 and '95, when Michael Jordan was retired and pursuing a baseball career), that was incredible for me and for the city. But the two that we won, we didn't have to play the Bulls [with Jordan], and you can't help but wonder if maybe that is why we won them. Hey, you never know, the game is funny that way sometimes—sometimes the best players don't win, sometimes the best players do win. If you look at that Rockets team, we were pretty good; you'd have to give them a chance, at least, against Michael and the Bulls. It's a team game—it's not about any one individual—it's how that team plays together.

When he came back for the Wizards and played those couple of years, that was fun for me personally; to be able to play against him after watching him for so many years. He was not the Chicago Bulls version of Michael Jordan, of course, but he was still good. And if he beat you, he was going to make sure you heard about it. It was an honor to be on the same court as a player you grew up trying to be like. Even now when I see him and I shake his hand or talk to him, it is something where you know how much of an honor it is. He changed the game for all of us.

Danny Green

Guard

Career: 2010–Present
Career Highlights: .... 2014 NBA Finals Champion

Green grew up on Long Island, and though he was in Knicks country, he was undeniably a Jordan fan. He has appeared in two NBA Finals with the Spurs.

I WAS A BIG Michael Jordan fan growing up. My dad was important to me, and he was also a big Michael Jordan fan, so I would watch basketball with him and I would root for the teams and players he liked—and Jordan was his favorite. So I got to be a big Jordan fan

through him. My dad was the one who put a basketball in my hands for the first time, so I learned from a young age that I wanted to be like Michael Jordan. We had a hoop in the yard, and I was out there trying to dunk all the time. My dad painted a court out there, and I would be out trying to do the things Michael Jordan did. I think every little kid at the time did.

In the '90s they won a lot of championships, I remember all of those later ones; I was eight or nine years old when they beat Seattle [in 1996]. They were always on TV, and of course, Michael was doing things on the court that had not been done before. It was always a lot of fun to watch. He was the greatest of all-time, too, so it was easy to root for him. Growing up, I watched them [the Bulls] a lot; I was not a Knicks fan at all even though I grew up in Knicks territory.[1] But I was a fan of certain players, and Michael Jordan was at the top of that list.

It's funny; I went to North Carolina, I rooted for the Tar Heels since I was something like twelve. That was where Michael Jordan went, so, I mean, who would not want to go there? I remember that Roy Williams came to my house on Long Island to recruit me, and it was all really exciting, but I had wanted to go to North Carolina all along. He really didn't even need to recruit me.

Now I am in a position where I went to North Carolina, went to the Final Four, and won a National Championship. Like Michael Jordan did. And now I get to play for a great organization, with Hall of Fame players, and go to the NBA Finals, like Michael Jordan did. It is weird to be in that position; a dream come true. It's a lot like what I used to watch on TV, except I get to live it.

---

[1] Green was born and raised in Long Island, New York.

Jay Williams

Guard

College Career: Duke University.............................2000–2002
College Highlights: ....NCAA AP Player of the Year, John R. Wooden Award, Naismith Men's College Player of the Year
NBA Career: 2003

Michael Jordan vs. Jay Williams										
Regular Season	Games	Wins	Losses	Win %	Field Goal %	PPG	Points (High)	RPG	APG	SPG
Jordan	3	3	0	100	38.1	13.7	17 (3/1/03)	7.7	6.7	1.0
Williams	3	0	3	0.0	9.1	1.7	3 (1/2/03)	1.0	3.7	0.3

Williams was the No. 2 pick in the draft by the Bulls out of Duke in 2002 and caused a bit of a ruckus in Chicago when he decided to occupy Jordan's corner locker at the United Center in his rookie year. Williams' career was cut short by a motorcycle accident, but his connection to Jordan lingered.

I FIRST BECAME A big fan of Michael Jordan during his battles with Isiah Thomas. Those were great series and made me want to be a basketball player. I could always relate more to Isiah, but I really wanted to be like Michael. I was infatuated with both of them, not only as player but as competitors. Today, it is a different age, players are more friendly with each other. I would never think for one second to extend my hand to someone on another team to help them up. I was always uber-competitive when I would cross those lines, and that is what I learned watching Michael Jordan battling Isiah Thomas. That's why I was infatuated with that rivalry—the ability to mentally take yourself to a different level.

I grew up in New Jersey, but had Michael Jordan posters and jerseys and all of that growing up. I definitely tried to shoot with my tongue out, you know, to be like him. It is a sign of his greatness that so many people have tried to imitate him. But he has so many moments that stand out: the shot he hit against the Utah Jazz at the foul line, the game against Portland where he made all those 3s and just shrugged, the shot against Cleveland to win that series. Those are the things that stand out.

What was most impressive, though, was that he brought the same mentality to every game. In the NBA Finals or playing against an expansion team, he had the same mentality. As a kid watching him, every single game, he was engaged. He wanted to dominate and prove to you he was the dominant force.

For me, it was a dream come true to be drafted by the Bulls because I was such a fan of his growing up. They took me with the No. 2 pick in that draft [2002], and my mentality was, we needed to move on, we needed to become a great team in our own right. When I got to Chicago, one of the first things I did was, I took MJ's locker. Someone told me, that's Jordan's locker, nobody has sat in it since. I said, "Well, I will take it, then."

I caught a ton of flak for that. But my whole thing was, how could I not want to be that close to greatness if it's right there? Nobody had sat in that locker since Jordan, so why not sit in the same locker that Michael sat in? I don't think it was disrespect, I thought it was the opposite, it was respect. It was a huge, huge moment for me, even though I got killed in the media for it. Who has the chance to say they took over Michael Jordan's locker in Chicago? I was not saying I was as good as Michael Jordan—that is how people took it. Look, I knew I was nowhere close to that, I was not trying to be that. I thought it was a huge opportunity. It was one of those things where no one was sitting there because they were intimidated. I wanted to show I was not intimidated. Why not?

I am a competitive person. I know I messed up in terms of my basketball career.[2] But I am still competitive now like I was then, I always want to get better. That has always been my mindset. So that was the competitive nature within myself with the Bulls—we were a team, and we were in the shadow of Michael Jordan. But he had been gone for four years. We needed to find our own identity, and my thought was that maybe that could be the first step in making that happen. I don't know whether that was the right thing to do or not, because I never got to find out how that would have played out.

What people did not know was that Michael and I had a little bit of relationship before I went to Chicago, because of the whole North Carolina–Duke thing. He would joke with me—he was playing with the Wizards at the time. He told me I would be the only Duke player he would consider drafting if I had come out my sophomore year, when Washington had the first pick [in 2001]. So during that season, I was taking a lot of criticism, I had taken MJ's locker. I was getting on my teammates publicly, trying to motivate them. Some people were killing me for it. But Michael called me and told me I was doing the right thing, that I needed to be a leader.

Now, that year, he had come back to play for Washington, that was his first year back on the court. I know Michael always talked about playing when he was angry—he liked it better—and that is the way I was. When I was angry, I would get a lot more out of myself on the court. So he came back with the Wizards and his first game in Chicago against the Bulls, it was after the New Year, in 2003, we were at the United Center. Michael got a fifteen-minute standing ovation from the fans there.

---

[2] Williams suffered a career-ending injury when he crashed his motorcycle in Chicago in June 2003.

I understood that the fans wanted to show their appreciation, of course I get that. But to be honest, it made me mad; an opposing player getting that much love in our building. I am not comparing myself to Michael, but just imagine if that was a young Michael Jordan in my shoes. If he was watching, say, Julius Erving in 1984 come through, and Julius Erving got a fifteen-minute ovation from Chicago fans, don't you think Michael Jordan would be pissed off about that? I respect Michael Jordan more than any other basketball player in the world, but that would not stop me from wanting to rip his head off on the court.

Was I able to do that? No, definitely not, because Michael Jordan was still, even at that age, better than I was and way more experienced. He scored on me multiple times in that game. He was older, but he was still really, really smart with the way he played. He would post you up, then he would actually tell me what he was about to do, and just like that, he would do it and score. He did that to me. He talked to me the whole game. It pissed me off, but I liked that, because he was just going at me. There was no friendship or anything, it was just competition.

I struggled with my shooting in that game. But after the game was over, he pulled me over and said, "Hey man, you keep up the fight. You fought me out there, you clawed me, every possession. You keep doing that and that is going to help you down the line." Coming from some-body like that, somebody who made it so big by doing that, that meant a lot to me. Because that's how he made it. He fought and clawed on every single possession, he refused to be told he was not good enough or that there were things he was not going to be able to do. Little things like that always stick with me with all that has happened, because that goes beyond basketball. That's about life. That's how you become successful and overcome adversity.

But all that is not really what stands out to me about Michael. The thing that really tells you what you need to know about him was what happened after my accident. Once I started to get healthy again, I was going to try to make a comeback in the NBA. I was working out every day one summer with Tim Grover at Hoops.[3] I always told Tim that I was dedicated to the comeback, to the point I wanted to be the first one in the gym every day and the last one to leave. I remember, he just kind of smiled at that. Because he knew that was not going to happen.

Every day I would come in early, I would come in right when the sun was coming up, you name it. The person that I never beat, though, was the guy who had just retired from the Wizards—it was MJ. He was always the first one in the gym. He wasn't even playing anymore at that point. It was mind-blowing to me. But that dude was still in the gym, doing weight-lifting sessions at 6:30 in the morning. I would come in early, thinking I got him this time, but his car was always there.

It is strange to think about, but that was maybe the best summer of my life, even though I was not able to come back, I did not get back into the league. He would talk to me all the time, encourage me to keep coming back, to keep fighting, to keep pushing. Spending time with that guy was really eye-opening, getting a chance to know his personality and his work ethic—after his career was over. Because he worked really hard, and if he was that way after his career was over, how hard must he have worked when he was playing? I can't imagine who he was in the midst of his prime.

The best part though? He would still show no mercy. We would play, I might be having trouble with my leg or my breathing. I was still rehabbing. But he would still attack me the same way. He did not go easy on me just because I had gotten hurt. He just loves to compete, and that is what I needed. I did not want any pity from anybody. I want you to play the same way you would play if it was a Game 7. That was his mindset. He had a switch that never turned off. I will always appreciate that about him.

---

[3] Grover's old gym on Chicago's West Side, where Jordan also worked out.

Ray Allen

Guard

Career: 1997–Present
Career Highlights: .... 10-time All-Star, two-time NBA Finals
Champion

Regular Season	Games	Wins	Losses	Win %	Field Goal %	PPG	Points (High)	RPG	APG	SPG
Michael Jordan vs. Ray Allen										
Jordan	12	9	3	75.0	50.8	28.8	44 (1/298)	5.5	3.8	1.3
Allen	12	3	9	25.0	41.3	16.7	27 (1/16/98)	5.0	3.5	1.2

Allen was a star at Connecticut and signed with Jordan's shoe brand after college. He has gone on to have an incredibly durable—and certainly worthy of the Hall of Fame—career, playing for 18 seasons and earning 10 All-Star selections.

I SIGNED WITH THE new Brand Jordan right out of college. I was a junior at UConn when I entered the draft, and I met with Michael and they wanted me to wear their shoes. That was something that was just really exciting for me because I grew up—like everyone else—watching Michael Jordan and seeing his career, watching him closely, seeing what a winner he was and wanting to be like that. But I mean, in my childhood, I could not afford to run out and buy a pair of Jordan's. I wanted them, but I was not going to be able to afford them. So to be asked to represent that brand as a guy just coming into the NBA, it was something that I was really excited about and it was great because it brought back all the memories of watching Michael when I was a kid. But the brand has grown so much now, you see players in all sports wearing them. The Jumpman logo, it's everywhere now.

You know, there were two parts of watching him when you were a kid. Everybody watched those dunk contests and saw what he did, and it was amazing. It's the kind of thing that does stick with you, when you are out there practicing, it is sort of burned in your memory and you want to do things like that. I mean, I was a kid; it was not like I would run out and try to dunk like that. All the players now, and not just the ones my age, they have seen what he did in those dunk contests in the '80s and all of that, and it is something that makes you want to do those kinds of things, to achieve that kind of greatness and athleticism. That's why they replay them all the time. For me, watching it as a kid, it always was in my mind when I would practice.

But there were also the great moments he had in those playoff series and the Finals, all those famous moments and the big shots he hit. When you watch those and you become a player in the NBA, you start to realize how hard that is to do, how often he made those kinds of shots. That takes a lot of focus and the willingness to put yourself out there. If you miss, it's all on you, you know? But he never shied away from those situations, and when you get to the NBA and realize how hard it is to do things like that, you really do appreciate it more. That's real greatness. As a child, those were some of my favorite memories, being a fan of MJ and the things he did in the playoffs and the Finals, and those are the things that will stand out in my mind for the rest of my life.

Derek Anderson

Guard/Forward

Career: 1998–2008
Career Highlights: .... 2006 NBA Finals Champion

Michael Jordan vs. Derek Anderson										
Regular Season	Games	Wins	Losses	Win %	Field Goal %	PPG	Points (High)	RPG	APG	SPG
Jordan	4	2	2	50.0	48.6	21.3	27 (11/15/97)	4.5	3.3	1.5
Anderson	4	2	2	50.0	38.1	9.0	14 (12/10/02)	2.3	3.8	0.5

Anderson's long association with Jordan began when he was drafted in 1997, becoming one of the first athletes to wear Jordan's new line of shoes. Anderson played 11 seasons in the NBA, appearing in 615 games—including one, just six games into his career, in which he had to guard Jordan.

WHEN I WAS a senior at Kentucky—without knowing in advance—Michael Jordan sent someone to look at me. He was sort of scouting me in a way; to join up with the new line of shoes and clothes, the Brand Jordan line. I had gone through some stuff with my knee injury,[4] but I had a good

---

[4] Anderson tore his ACL during his senior season at Kentucky but was still chosen by Cleveland with the 13th overall pick.

college career and they liked me. They came in and checked to see that I was healthy, saw that I did not have a bad attitude, and found out what kind of person I am. He recruited me, basically, and liked how I conducted myself, which is why he signed me. He said, "I see how you handle adversity, how positive you are, and I think you can do some things."

And so, I was one of the first five players that Brand Jordan ever signed. Michael was still playing, but it was obvious that he was planning for his future [after basketball] and all of that. It was great that he picked me out and I got a lifelong contract. That was before I had really even started my NBA career; they just liked how I carried myself.

But I still had to play against him. That was tough. I was healthy and young then, so I was ready for it. You have to compare now to then, if you were a top-notch shooting guard. Now, I would be one of the top five two-guards in the NBA, it is just not a big position in the league anymore. But back then? You had Michael Jordan, Reggie Miller, Allan Houston, Mitch Richmond, Latrell Sprewell, Ray Allen, Michael Finley, Vince Carter . . . it is a long list. We had two-guards for days. If you were a two-guard in the league at that time, it seemed like, man, every night was going to be a challenge defensively.

There were a lot of Hall of Famers at my position then, but definitely, Michael was the best. Him and Mitch Richmond—Mitch was always tough to guard, because he was strong, smart, and could post up. But Michael was the real challenge, obviously. The one you measured yourself against. I remember coming in as a rookie, I had signed with his brand and everything, and I was maybe two weeks into my career. But we beat Chicago, the first time we played them, in Cleveland my rookie year. I had a pretty good game, I guess, but it was just amazing beating those guys, because that was the time when, it seemed like, they just did not lose.[5]

---

[5] In twenty-two minutes, Derek scored six points with two assists and one rebound.

I was able to keep up with Michael in that game, defensively.[6] It was more or less my speed, because I was quick. I knew he did not want to go left, so I could beat him to his spots and do the best I could to make him take shots he did not want to take. I studied the game; I studied tape all the time, and I knew Mike likes to go right—like Kobe Bryant—he wants to go right and you know it, so you just have to figure out how to stop him.

I would take charges on those guys all the time because of my speed. I might not shut you down, but I am going to make you do something you are not comfortable with. You are going to have to make special plays all night long, because I am not going to let you into your comfort zone where you can destroy me. With a guy like Michael Jordan, that has to be your strategy.

I did retire after I won a championship with the Heat in '06. That's when Michael called me; he was running things in Charlotte at the time. I would not say we were friends, but we had a good business friendship, we had a good relationship that way—I don't do all the things he is famous for doing: I don't golf, I don't gamble, none of that. But I think he always respected me, and we are always willing to help each other with our camps or whatever it may be.

So, it was winter that year, the season was already going and I was already working on some different things in my career. I was thirty-two, I thought I was done with basketball, I thought I could sit on the couch for a little while. I was still in shape, but I was retired. I got a call from Charlotte, so I answered it and someone was saying, "MJ would like to talk to you." I am like, "Oh, really?"

He tells me he wants me to come in and help his team out, be a veteran on the bench and help out with the younger players. I figured that sounded pretty good. I could come in, sit on the bench, no pressure on me to score, I can tutor and mentor the young guys—Raymond Felton, Gerald Wallace, guys like that. They had a good young team,

---

[6] Jordan finished with 19 points on 7-for-17 shooting from the field.

but they needed some leadership. I was a veteran and wasn't looking for any kind of big contract or anything.

Sure enough, maybe two weeks later, I'm in the starting lineup. I was thinking, *Oh, man. This is not what I signed up for.* But it's Michael Jordan and I was not going to say no to him. He was really good to me when I came into the league and was starting my career, so I was going to help him if I could there at the end of my career. I did that for two years, and that was enough. But that's how life goes—if you treat people well, they'll treat you well back. It comes full circle.

Jermaine O'Neal

Forward/Center

Career: 1997–Present
Career Highlights: ....six-time All-Star,
2002 Most Improved Player

Michael Jordan vs. Jermaine O'Neal										
Regular Season	Games	Wins	Losses	Win %	Field Goal %	PPG	Points (High)	RPG	APG	SPG
Jordan	11	6	5	54.5	44.2	26.6	41 (1/4/03)	5.0	3.5	1.5
O'Neal	11	5	6	45.5	46.2	12.9	27 (11/22/01)	7.9	1.2	0.3

O'Neal came into the league as Jordan's career was winding down. He entered the league straight out of high school and was drafted by the

Portland Trail Blazers in 1996. He was traded to the Indiana Pacers in 2000 and then made the NBA All-Star Team six consecutive seasons. He played on the same All-Star team as Jordan when Jordan was with the Washington Wizards.

I **WASN'T A BIG** basketball fan growing up, and I think the first games that I started watching were when the Lakers and Bulls played each other in the NBA Finals in 1991. The play I remember most was in the Chicago Stadium when he switched hands as he went up to the rim in that game against the Lakers. His greatness was next to none. To be able to play against him, and then play with him in the All-Star Games, was a dream come true. I still remember the "I want to be like Mike" commercials. That is my favorite memory of Michael.

We were at shoot around here [in the United Center] and were all talking about Michael Jordan and saying how it would feel to hold him to 25 points and feel like it was a success. I have a fourteen-year-old and a seven-year-old who obviously never saw Michael play, but they both know who Michael Jordan is. You can pick any memory and get one hell of a story to go behind it.

When I was in Portland, he did an interview before the game and talked about how he had to worry about me in the game. He gave me some love that day. He also signed his last pair of All-Star shoes for me.

Greg Buckner

Guard/Forward

Career: **2000–2009**

Michael Jordan vs. Greg Buckner										
Regular Season	Games	Wins	Losses	Win %	Field Goal %	PPG	Points (High)	RPG	APG	SPG
Jordan	5	0	5	0.0	41.1	17.0	25 (1/18/03)	4.2	4.2	1.4
Buckner	5	5	0	100	52.2	6.0	16 (11/17/02)	4.4	1.2	1.8

Buckner is one of the few players who can say that, in five games against Jordan, he never lost. He played 10 seasons for five different teams, but one of the standout memories Buckner has is guarding Jordan in his final game, in Philadelphia in 2003.

WHAT'S UNBELIEVABLE **IS** that I was the last one to guard him. Last time he was ever in an NBA game, I was on him, I was the last defender he faced. When I look back, I think about it all the time, *Why didn't I keep the program or the game notes or the ticket?* Something like that, just to have that memento. I mean, it was part of history and I was there, guarding the guy. But it is amazing to be on the same court with a player like that, the best player ever, and to be the last person to guard him and to watch him at the end of the game, everybody wanted to hug him, shake his hand, and talk to him. He was forty years old, and he was playing for the Wizards and not the Bulls and all of that. But still, it was Michael Jordan.

But I did not keep a single thing from that game. When you're young, you don't quite realize the significance. I mean, I understood it was Michael Jordan and all, but I was not thinking, *This is something where I am going to want to keep everything I can and have it forever.* You're young and you think something like that might happen every day. Honestly, once or twice a year I think about that night. I did not even get an autograph from him, I didn't take a picture with him. It is crazy that I never thought to do that.

He was older then but he was still Michael Jordan. Everybody idolized him at that stage of his career. No matter who you were or how good you were, everybody idolized him because they knew what he did for the league and for all of us players and for basketball in general. He was still capable of putting up some points at the time, he had some big scoring games in those years in Washington, so your defense still had to be aware of him. He was more of a post-up player, but he was really smart so he could take advantage of you if you slept on him.

And, mentally, he was still trying to take advantage of everyone. For my career, I always tried to approach guarding him the same way: just focus on the game plan, focus on guarding him in the post, and keep your mouth shut. That is the big thing. Do not get into it with him, because you're going to lose. And I knew that is how he gets himself going. The first time I played against him, that is what I was told, just don't start talking with him, because there is a long line of stories about guys who talked noise to Michael Jordan and he winds up going out and scoring 40 in a row or whatever it might be.

There was one game, we were playing against them, and he was off to a slow start and you could tell he wanted to get going. He was trying to motivate himself. So he was talking noise to me—talking noise, talking noise, nonstop. I was out there and I heard the whole game was, "Buck! Hey, Buck!" I just told myself, *He is trying to get in your head. Do not to let that happen.* Because if you talk back to him, he is going to get his lather going and he will try to destroy you. He kept shouting it, "Buck! Buck!"

I smiled and I told him, "I am not listening to you. I saw what you've done to all those other guys. I heard the stories." I was not going to be a part of that. I didn't want to become one of those stories. And I don't think he ever really got going in the game.

But that last game in Philadelphia, obviously, that was different. I remember, as the game was winding down, we had a big lead and Michael was on the bench, but everybody in the stands was chanting for him, they all wanted Doug Collins to put him back in the game just for one more stretch. Everybody was cheering for him, going, "We want Mike!"

They were not going to the playoffs, you knew it was his last game, it wasn't like, "Maybe they will get hot in the playoffs, let's see what happens." You knew that was Michael Jordan's last minutes on the court, ever. So you just got to give a guy like that the respect he deserves. As time was winding down, he got a standing ovation from the fans in Philadelphia, from his teammates, from us on the Sixers. He deserved it.

If I remember right, there was a little more than two minutes to play and Larry Brown, he was coaching us and he is a Carolina guy and a smart guy, so he knew the significance of getting Michael back out on the floor and letting him finish out on a positive note, getting a dead-ball situation so he could get that ovation from the fans. He wanted us to foul him, and we did. We went to grab Michael in the backcourt so he could go to the line and go out that way.[7]

It was an amazing experience. You just have to be blessed and lucky to be in a situation like that. I just wish I had kept something from that game.

---

[7] Jordan had checked into the game with 2:35 to play, and after making the free throws, checked back out at 1:44.

Jabari Parker

Forward

NBA Career: ....Drafted 2nd overall in the 2014 NBA Draft

Parker, a star forward out of Chicago in the mold of Derrick Rose and Dwyane Wade, starred at Duke for one year before entering the draft and going to Milwaukee with the second pick. Before he was picked by Milwaukee, though, Parker was signed as an endorser by Brand Jordan.

I MET HIM WHEN I was much younger. He is someone I idolized when I was growing up, and even now, he is someone I want to be

like in my career. Once you think of the Bulls—and I was a Bulls fan growing up—you think of Mr. Jordan. I was most definitely a fan of his when I was young and just coming up, even though I was not really able to watch him in his prime. But that is how it is in Chicago. Once you establish yourself, you will always get a certain amount of respect, whether it is Michael Jordan or Dwyane Wade or guys from other sports. That is what I am hoping to accomplish.

So it was an easy decision to sign with the Jordan Brand. It has been good because I know they're very family-oriented.

When you sign with the Jordan Brand, you are around some good teams, good people, and a clean image. When I was going through the recruiting process with different shoe companies, that was the one I was leaning toward all the way, being from Chicago and it being Mr. Jordan. They were definitely most appealing in that recruiting process for me.